"I Grew Up Listening to You"

People tell me...

"I Grew Up Listening to You"

Stories From Behind the Mic

Tommy Edwards

You May Know Him As Li'l Tommy from Animal Stories^{SM}

Paperback ISBN: 9781658810395

Printed in the United States of America

Book Design: Creative Publishing Book Design

I dedicate this book to my family. My mom Thelma, dad Carl, brother Jack and sister JoJo and their families. And especially Mary Lou, my love, along with our children Shannon, Amy, Tommy and our grandchildren

Contents

Introduction

I ADMIT I'VE BEEN VERY LUCKY. I HAVE A WONDERFUL family and a wonderful life. I've worked with incredible talent on the radio and done more than my share of playing practical jokes on the people I've worked with. I've been the victim of those antics too, while I was broadcasting, and did my best to keep from laughing or being distracted while the naked dancing girls were doing their best to confuse me. If it sounded like we were having a good time on the radio, imagine what was really going on in the studio or in the next studio. I'll share what I can remember along with some stories about another side of our *charming and delightful old friend.*

I've been in the presence of military power while working in The Pentagon and handling highly classified material. Some decisions I witnessed are now in history books. I've been in the presence of incredible athletic talent with the Chicago Bulls of the NBA and I've contributed ideas that have lasted in game presentation throughout sports.

1

I've met fascinating people in music, broadcasting, sports and even the underworld! My career has taken me to prestigious addresses on Broadway, Michigan Avenue and Sunset Boulevard. The achievements I've earned are light-years away from the goals I set for myself as a younger fellow. To say I've been fortunate is an understatement.

Radio is a small world. I continue to follow the careers of people I have worked with and I am proud that I shared a moment of their history. I wish them well and if I get the chance to see them again, I'd love to hear their radio stories because every station has them; every radio person has lived them.

I've been blessed with a wonderful family. I love and married a girl that has shared everything with me. We have three children who, after graduating college, pursued careers in broadcasting. We have four beautiful grandchildren that give us the opportunity to attend Little League baseball games, school musicals and theater performances.

I always dreamed of being on the radio. And as a teen I eventually did get to live that dream in the town where I grew up. I'd listen to air-checks of major market talent and I wanted to join them. But joining big-time jocks on big-time stations was just another big-time dream. It was a fantasy that I thought would never happen. But it did. Indeed, I was lucky to live it.

I don't want to forget where it all started and how it happened. A long time ago I read a book by legendary TV Newsman Harry Reasoner titled *Before the Colors Fade* and that title and story have stayed with me. Reasoner wrote about the early days of television journalism and his role in it. My intention was to compile some stories in a file so my children and grandchildren could read about some of the crazy things their mother/grandmother and I did. Hopefully in the end they will see that in our 50+ years together, we lived our dream and we want them to live theirs.

There's no question that this book wouldn't have been published without Mary Lou's encouragement. When I began sharing these stories with her, she encouraged me to write more. She offered to be a proofreader and helped me recall the stories and memories we experienced together. She kept reminding me of the hundreds of times people would tell me they grew up listening to me. It is truly something I've heard regularly over the last several decades. In fact, over the last 10 years or so I've also heard "my **mother** grew-up listening to you" and even "my **grandfather** says he loved listening to you and Uncle Lar'." I think all of us who have spent a lifetime on the radio cherish comments like that from people who said we had a small part in their lives. I know I find it very rewarding.

Here are a number of stories that are all true – at least the way I remember them! I want to thank Al Rosen, Jim Smith, Judy Mayer Rosen, Ed Marcin, Jim Kerr, Scott Zolke, Marty Greenberg, Bob Sirott, John Landecker, Rick Novak, Michelle McComas and Dave Van Dyke for helping me to rekindle or confirm a memory or two. Special thanks to Shannon and Pat Bobillo, Amy and Brendan Smith, Tommy Grimes and especially Mary Lou for your love and support. There are so many friends I've met and worked with over the years. I am grateful and feel privileged that many of them are still good friends.

And one more thing: Since I played music on the radio my whole career, certain songs popped into my head as I wrote each chapter. Just for fun I've included the titles of a few of them.

CHAPTER 1

A Kid with a Daydream

"Peggy Sue" – Buddy Holly
"Heartbreak Hotel" – Elvis Presley
"I Only Have Eyes for You" – The Flamingos

Every young boy who loves sports, dreams of being the player who makes the winning shot just as the buzzer goes off. I had that dream over and over out on the driveway even when it was getting too dark to see the basket.

In my room it was a different daydream. And I had the same daydream almost every night I can remember. It was being on the radio playing all those great songs and having a good time. I would be listening to the radio while I imagined what it would be like to be in a radio studio and having thousands of listeners tuned in. But the most important listeners would be the girls in my class at school. I'd be a hero. It was my chance to be a star.

My goal was to be on the radio in my hometown: Topeka, Kansas. I didn't dare imagine myself working in a big city like Kansas City.

So how did I get to live that dream and be successful in New York City, Chicago and Los Angeles? It all started in the basement of our house on Mulvane Street thanks to my mother's vacuum hose (which was my microphone), my 45-rpm record player and some Elvis Presley records.

My mother was always very tolerant and supportive of my deejay fantasy. She always knew where the vacuum was, and she never complained. She was my one and only listener in the house.

My parents, Carl and Thelma, were older than the parents of most of my friends. Mom was 40 years old when she had me – 42 when she had my little brother, Jack. My sister JoAnne was a teenager at that time. My father was in his mid-40s when I was born and working for Boeing Aircraft in Wichita, Kansas. We moved to Topeka when I was a toddler. There, Dad worked as an appliance salesman and I can recall how he'd always come home from the store in the early evening exhausted from standing on his feet all day. Then he would pack up the family in our 1949 black Chevrolet and drive around various neighborhoods looking for homes without a television antenna on their roof. My brother Jack and I would make it a game to see who could spot them first. When we found one, we would stay in the car and Dad would knock on the door to invite the owners to our house to see what television was all about. We had one of the first TVs in Topeka. Mom would set up chairs in the living room so the future customers could watch the programming sign-on and eventually sign-off. Television stations were only on the air at night. This was a system that worked. Dad sold many televisions.

Mom's primary job was taking care of my brother and me. Occasionally she worked part-time at a friend's clothing store whenever she was needed. She was a Den Mother when I was in Cub Scouts and later a Sunday School Teacher. She wasn't overly religious, but I knew she had a very close relationship with God. We never missed a Sunday at Church.

In the late 1980's I videotaped an interview with my mom and the oldest members of our family about their earliest memories. I spoke with my mother and her sisters, Mary Lois and Anne who were all in their 80s at that time. My Auntie Anne said she remembered traveling from Ohio to Kansas in a covered wagon when she was a little girl. Auntie "O" (Mary Lois) told me a story about how their father, Clair (my grandfather), raised hogs on a farm. His prized boar was named **Buster Black**. And my mother described how she and Auntie Anne taught school in a one-room schoolhouse.

My earliest memory is my mother, father, little brother Jack and me moving from Topeka to Tacoma, Washington when I was in the 1st grade. By that time my sister JoAnne was married with a home in Topeka.

I can recall, while living in Tacoma, walking to school each day with a couple of girls who lived in the neighborhood. I can still picture the scenic walk where we could see Puget Sound in the distance and Mount Rainier's snowcapped peak. My father, Carl, worked for Boeing making machine gun parts for B-52 aircraft. He taught Jack and me how to fish off a pier on Puget Sound. I remember my mother bundled up and freezing while she watched us get frustrated because everyone else was catching fish except us. She never complained.

We returned to Topeka the following year because my parents were homesick. Both sides of the family had relatives in and near the city. We moved into an apartment on the upper floor of a house on 10th Street and I started attending Lowman Hill School. My brother Jack came down with rheumatic fever and was bedridden for a full year. I knew how difficult it was for him not being able to be outside playing ball with us. I spent as much time as I could telling him stories about what happened in school. We'd laugh about some of the silly things. And I spent the early evening sitting with him watching TV. After Jack's recovery, my parents bought a house on Mulvane Street that I lived in until I left for the Navy in 1966.

The basement was my make-believe radio studio. I previously mentioned that I used the vacuum hose as a microphone. I put one end into an opening of the huge furnace (my transmitter) and used my 45 rpm record player as my turntable. I'd talk into the end of the hose then play a song and put the end of the hose next to the record player's speaker. I'd often run upstairs and ask my mother how it sounded and she always said she enjoyed the music. I realized later there's no way she could have heard anything. She was just being my Mom. For newscasts I would read stories out of the Topeka newspaper. I was also spending an enormous amount of time listening to KTOP radio in my room to songs by the Shirelles, The Crests, Elvis Presley, Little Richard, Jerry Lee Lewis and so many more. I practiced identifying songs as soon as they came on the radio and practiced a talk-up to the vocal – which means talking over the instrumental beginning of a song and stopping just as the singing begins.

While I was a student at Boswell Junior High School, I entered talent contests with a Jerry Mahoney ventriloquist doll and practiced throwing my voice. I was also in the boys' choir and I guess it was here I was getting comfortable with being on stage.

One summer Jack and I were sent to our uncle's ranch/farm in Del Norte, Colorado. My uncle Glen was one of my mother's brothers and he had a rather large amount of land. We worked on the farm for a full summer and it was a wonderful experience. We were riding horses every day. Sometimes we rode horseback over the Rio Grande River. My uncle had us opening irrigation channels in the fields, milking cows each morning, feeding chickens and riding horses to an area where a herd of cattle were grazing so we could check on the health of newborn calves. Calves gonna be OK, Uncle Glen?

Other summers back in Topeka were spent fishing each day at a large pond about a mile from our house and weekends at Lake Shawnee. Some days we'd take our rifles down to the river and shoot at targets. Our father had previously arranged to have Jack and me attend a Topeka Police training program on firearm safety with .22 caliber rifles. We spent a lot of time at the police firing range and I got to be pretty good. In fact, years later at Navy boot camp in San Diego, the weapons instructor said he could tell I had training because, as he put it, I was a marksman.

In high school I tried out for a role in the classic play *Laura* which had starred Gene Tierney in the 1944 film production. My role was very minor, but I was in the very first scene of the play. It was my first taste of acting and I loved it.

In my junior year I had secondary roles in musicals like *South Pacific* and *Flower Drum Song* and worked on stage crew of various productions.

It was in my senior year I was cast as Elwood P. Dowd in *Harvey*. This was the performance that I am most proud of in high school. The drama teacher who produced and directed all of the performances was the most influential teacher of my life. Martha Herrick coached, pushed, inspired and urged me to bring some creative efforts to the role. That gave me confidence in my skills and let me express some of my personality in the character. Her lessons stayed with me throughout my radio career. I'll never forget my father telling me he was proud of me when he came up on stage after the performance.

One of the other students who I became friends with when I first started in drama was John Walquist. Johnny was two years older and was on the radio after school as a newsman at KTOP. During the summer between my sophomore and junior year, I contacted Johnny and asked if I could come to the radio station to watch him work. He checked with his boss and obviously put in a good word for me because I not only had the chance to watch Johnny work but everyone else at the station as well. I became an unpaid go-fer around the radio station, getting coffee or lunch from a drive-in restaurant for anyone who wanted it. I didn't mind not being paid. I was watching how everything happens.

Finally, I was hired in my Junior year. I was going to make $1.05 per hour watching the teletype machine and listening to the police and sheriff radios every weekend. I got my big break one weekend when a bulletin came across the teletype, and I couldn't find anyone to read it. I called the Program Director and he told me to read it myself. I couldn't believe it. I was going to read the bulletin on the air! I immediately got very nervous. Do I use my regular voice or my "announcer" voice? I rehearsed that short bulletin at least 20 times. Before I told the DJ I had a bulletin to read on the air, I called my parents, my sister, my aunts and anyone else I could think of to turn on the radio and listen for a surprise! I must have done a good job because the Program Director called and told me to do a 10-minute newscast that night on the FM radio station. That became a weekly assignment and during the next two years I worked after school in the news department and eventually on-air with a weekly music show.

Someone whose work I admired and respected before I got my first job in radio, was a KTOP DJ. He went by the name of Tony Kurtis and his line was: "I'm Tony Kurtis, spelled with a 'K' if we may – K for Kurtis and Kurtis for K-TOP." He was so smooth on the air and the way he talked about the music was a step above what everybody else was saying. By the time I started at KTOP, Kurtis had already moved on. He later attended Law School at Washburn University while doing the evening news on the local TV station, WIBW-TV. He went on to be a national figure and highly respected journalist after he received his law degree. By this time, he used his real name Bill Kurtis. Bill and I connected later working on various telethons in Chicago.

Topeka was a great place to grow up. I had a number of child-hood friends that remained good friends all the way through high school, college and to this day. Even in elementary school I dreamed about being on the radio. KTOP radio at 1490 kHz was the one station I listened to most. Sometimes I'd listen to WHB in Kansas City – especially at night. Also at night I'd tune into KOMA in Oklahoma City and XERF in Mexico with Wolfman Jack. I loved listening to AM radio stations from far away late at night. I didn't start listening to WLS until 1960 when they flipped to Top 40. It was then I fell in love with The Big 89 out of Chicago. The music and the DJ voices sounded so much bigger and better than KTOP.

I repeated what the WLS DJs said, and I pictured what their studio must look like. It had to be bigger than KTOP's. WLS was much more powerful than KTOP. It was the best radio station on the air. I never dreamed I'd work there some day.

CHAPTER 2

My First Job in Radio

"Runaway" – Del Shannon
"Only the Lonely" – Roy Orbison
"He's So Fine" – The Chiffons

I HAD SUCH A VALUABLE EDUCATIONAL EXPERIENCE at KTOP-AM. The radio station was located in North Topeka on Buchanan Street. It was in a two-story house-like structure with a big gravel parking lot under a picture window. The radio tower was located out back in a large fenced in field. The two air-studios were upstairs separated by a glass window. In the AM studio was the 250 watt AM and one FM transmitter. We had only one set of main transmitters while most stations had two of each (so engineers could alternate their use to prolong their life cycle). The newsroom was on the second floor in the back of the building. The Associated Press teletypewriter was in a closet with sound suppression wallcoverings.

13

Out in the field where the radio tower was located, we had a donkey named Molly. She would graze on the grass, so the owners didn't have to mow it. One of my earliest jobs was to make sure Molly had enough water and a salt block. The radio station had a rule that no one was to go into the field except the Chief Engineer who was a son of the owner. One of the reasons people were forbidden to go into the field next to the radio tower was to avoid anyone getting RF (radiation or radio frequency) burns by touching the tower. The anti-collision beacons on the tower would burn out occasionally and the station would have to call a fellow whose job it was to travel the country climbing towers to replace bulbs. One of the duties of the night-time announcer would be to confirm that the tower lights were on and blinking.

The positioning statement was: "K-TOP RADIO ONE TOPEKA. THE KANSAS TOWER OF PERSONALITY." Later the station bought the PAMS Jingle package: BIG TOP. The jingles were: "K-TOP BIG TOP 1490 TOPEKA!"

Later KTOP hired a new Chief Engineer who was one of the more colorful characters I ever worked with. His first name was Grady and he was jokingly referred to as The Bully. He was a big strong middle-aged guy who threatened us by saying he would personally break the fingers of anyone who touched his equipment or tools. He was mostly bald with huge hands and always wore the same shirt and jeans. Subsequently in my career I learned that each station I worked for had a unique character who was most likely the Chief Engineer. Nothing happens at radio stations without the Chief Engineer knowing about it beforehand. They are involved in everything from arranging offices, changing telephones and even some things with the on-air talent. They knew about a hire or fire of any member of the air staff before it was announced. Plus, they held the FCC licenses and were locally responsible to uphold technical FCC rules and regulations.

In the 80s I met Max Tash, one of the producers of the television show *WKRP in CINCINNATI* at a wedding. I told him about Grady and mentioned to him they should have developed a character that represented those unique individuals that populated radio stations around the country. The show had DJs, managers, a receptionist and a secretary but no engineers. The TV show was already off the air by then but the producer seemed interested in my idea.

When I first joined KTOP, I had to have a restricted FCC license. Later I had to have a 3rd Class license. These credentials were necessary to take transmitter readings. In the early days of radio, readings had to be taken every half hour. Later it was once an hour, and today no license is required for announcers since transmitter readings are all automated. Some of the people I worked with *never* took transmitter readings. They would just copy the same numbers over and over when they were about to sign off their shift. I imagine the rule at that time was to ensure you didn't deviate your frequency to crowd someone else and to maintain the authorized power output.

During the years I was at KTOP, I learned most of what is expected in the profession. The air-personalities on the station were really good considering the station was only 250 watts and couldn't even be heard in some neighborhoods in the City of Topeka. The morning guy was Bob Barber. He came to Topeka from Baltimore and he called himself the Morning Mayor of Topeka. Bob Harris was the midday DJ and he became a very successful salesman. Afternoons were handled by the owner's son, Charles Axton who used the air name of Charlie Christian. And his *Charlie Christian K-TOP 40 Show* was highly successful as he was exceptionally talented. He used character voices and even had a Poet's Corner where he would use a British accent and read from humorous poetry books. Charlie had studied at the Juilliard Preparatory School in New York and the Kansas City Conservatory of Music. He went on to earn a Ph.D. from the University of Kansas and was a distinguished Director/Conductor of American Musicals in Germany. He was also a Guest Conductor for the Berlin Symphony Orchestra.

After Charlie left to pursue his career in music, the afternoon show was done by Smilin' Bill McCall who used drop-in sound effects throughout his show. This was very unusual at the time. The laugh tracks and sound effects were all on one giant ET (Electrical Transcription). An ET was a 16-inch record and Bill would cue up the sounds on one of the two giant turntables we had in the studio. One of his favorite tracks was a funny sounding giggle. Anytime he said something *he* thought was funny, he had his own laugh track. I always thought the giggle was funnier than what he said.

Nights were the domain of Johnny Dark. That wasn't his real name and I don't remember what it was but he was one of my favorite all time on-air jocks. He had a magnificent deep voice with a unique level of crispness to it. He'd work the microphone very close and kept one hand under his chin whenever he would speak. If he was going to do a slip-cue of the record, he'd stop talking just long enough to change hands under his chin. A slip-cue involved cueing up a record, holding it with your finger and then starting the turntable. Once you wanted the record to start, you'd release your finger on the record. Johnny had women calling him every night and some would show up at the station to see the man behind the sexy voice; he was a nighttime animal! Sometimes he'd radio me in the mobile unit on the two-way on my way to work and ask me to stop by the liquor store on the way in. I'd knock on the back door and the lady would bring a pint of Seagram's Blended Whiskey to me. He had an arrangement with the lady that he'd pay her later, but I had to meet her at the store's back door because I was still underage. Then he'd ask me to stop by a drive-in burger joint called King Karry Out and get him a large Coke. He'd mix the Seagram's with the Coke and drink it throughout his show.

Johnny had his favorite lines like: "I'm sick and tired of being tired and sick." And he would have lines with a sexy edge like "I'm looking for you Baby Doll in the Cadillac with the top down."

The overnight jock was Professor J. Jazzmo Bop. He was an older man, one of the very few African American DJs on the air in Topeka. Professor was a sweetheart. He'd bring his lunch to work the midnight – 6 a.m. shift. I really enjoyed hanging in the studio to watch and listen to him work. One of his favorite lines was: "This is Professor J. Jazzmo trust everybody but cut the cards yourself Bop." One Sunday night I asked him if he knew where I could buy some beer. I was underage and they didn't sell beer on Sundays in Kansas in those days. He picked up the phone and called a friend about a half mile from the radio station. He said that I'd be right down and to give me a six-pack of beer and Professor Bop would pay him later.

The Professor never took a vacation and he never called in sick. Then one afternoon he took us by surprise. He called to say he needed to take the night off. The manager asked for a volunteer to do the show that night. I remember before anyone could speak up I said, "I'll do it." He told me that's not possible since I was still in high school. I begged him for the chance. He said, "No, it is a school night and there's no way your parents will agree to it." I told him, "My parents know how much I want to do this, they won't object." He told me to get their permission and I knew that would be easy. My mother packed a thermos of coffee and several donuts for me and I was so nervous when I was on the air, I never touched them.

The manager told me he listened to part of my show and he liked what he heard. He offered me a regular weekend show. I couldn't believe it – I was still in high school and I was on the radio. It was my big break! Once I started college, I had my own daily show.

It's been my experience that there's one thing in common between major market radio stations and small market stations: Practical jokes. You'll read several examples of them later on. One at KTOP is very vivid in my memory and it makes me laugh every time I think of it.

While I was in high school, I read the 9:55 p.m. newscast every weeknight. The DJ on the air at the time was Johnny Dark. I would read a story or two and break for a commercial that Johnny would play from the air-studio. Sometimes he would ask me to take longer than five minutes to read the news and not throw a cue for a commercial so he could go downstairs to use the bathroom. The volume to the monitor in the unisex bathroom was controlled by the newsroom monitor. Johnny would on occasion walk into the newsroom during these long newscasts and throw a paper wad at me or try to distract me some way to make me laugh while I read the news. On this night I read the news for a few minutes and then said, "More news in a minute." I then turned the monitor all the way down so it sounded as if there was dead air to Johnny in the bathroom. I resumed reading the news. I remember hearing him yelling and cussing as he charged up the stairs on the way to Studio A while pulling up his pants. When he got to his studio and realized what I had done, he was furious. The next night he came into the newsroom while I was reading the news and since I couldn't see what he was doing, I thought he was urinating on my news copy. But what he actually did was fill his mouth up with water and he was squirting it out of his mouth and all over my news copy. I had to stop reading to stifle a laugh. It was impossible to keep from breaking up – it was priceless! This began a series of attempts to break each other up during our respective live reads. Fire extinguishers were sometimes used, low level sounds that couldn't be picked up by the microphones and even mini skits were performed just to try to make the other guy laugh.

On one occasion Johnny asked one of my fellow news people, Van Moe and the receptionist, Theresa, to help him pull a stunt on me while I read a 15-minute newscast on KTOP-FM. The FM station was pretty much automated playing huge tapes of background music and the only live programming was at 6 p.m. and again at 10 p.m. weekdays. The 6 o'clock news was 15 minutes of live read and the 10 p.m. news was only 5 minutes. Van convinced me to do my news at a stand-up microphone just like it's done in the 'big time' stations and he would run the board. So I agreed. Big mistake! As soon as I began to read, Theresa and Johnny started taking off my clothes. I couldn't react or stop reading because we all knew the owner listened every evening. First the shirt was unbuttoned and removed, my slacks were loosened and removed and eventually I got down to only my underwear and socks. Then when it was time for the weather forecast, Van turned the microphone off briefly while Theresa showered my backside with a CO_2 fire extinguisher spray. Needless to say it was extremely cold and the weather forecast was for hot temperatures. Imagine my shivering voice announcing temperatures in the 100s for tomorrow. I will say this however: I never broke up in laughter until the newscast was all over. I wasn't about to let them win!

I mentioned that KTOP-FM was mostly automated music since not too many people had an FM receiver. To promote KTOP-FM, the station ran a program on Sunday nights called *Stereo House*. I hosted the program by dragging a microphone with an extra-long cable from the AM studio to the FM studio placing the two microphones side-by-side. I would first have to turn the FM mic ON before the AM mic. When I finished introducing the album, I had to do the reverse. I turned the AM mic OFF first, then the FM mic all to avoid feedback. I'd ask listeners to put their AM radio on one side of the room and their FM radio on the other side of the room. Don't forget, in those days there were no AM/FM radios. They were two different devices.

Each week I would visit a particular record store and select stereo albums to feature on the program. One would be jazz, another would be a Broadway Show and the last would be classical music. The needles on the big turntables would be changed to stereo needles and one channel would be wired to be broadcast on KTOP-AM and the other on KTOP-FM. I would then run my announcements on the two mics in front of me and sweep my voice over the two mics whenever I said *Stereo House*.

KTOP was also the place I learned broadcast journalism on a very local level. I grew up in the news department and drove one of the mobile units to cover all the "breaking news" (I'm so tired of that term). Each mobile unit had a two-way radio connecting the car to the newsroom, Studio A and the receptionist's desk. Every single siren in the city created a news report on the air. We had direct telephone lines with the two ambulance companies who would call us whenever they were dispatched for whatever reason. They would tip us in the event of an accident in the city or on nearby rural roads, as well as fires, murders, shootings, a bridge collapse or anything else they were called to. The DJ on the air would then call me at home. If I was in bed, I'd get up, jump in the mobile unit that I drove every day and race to the scene to do a live report via two-way radio. I even had a police scanner in my personal car, and I'd hear police calls whenever I drove it around town. I didn't have a two-way radio in my car so I would have to use a public telephone (remember them?) to call in the report. I even had a police scanner in my bedroom for a while thinking I would hear important police calls while I was sleeping. Obviously, that didn't work – I heard the calls but got zero sleep.

I can still recall the very first murder I covered, the first suicide, the first small plane crash and the first train-car accident. All were gruesome sights that one never gets accustomed to. The first murder was of a woman who had been sexually assaulted and for some reason reporters were allowed on the murder scene during the police investigation. The reason I remember this is because the Kansas Bureau of Investigation had all of the reporters come in to be fingerprinted because there were a number of prints at the scene belonging to people other than the victim and police investigators. It was such a strange feeling walking through the apartment without any restrictions. There was broken furniture and a large stain on the living room rug. I'll never forget that sight. I learned a few years later that my fingerprints were already on file when I joined the Navy.

One of the most important news bulletins I have ever read on the air was the assassination of President John F. Kennedy.

On November 22, 1963 I was doing the midday show on KTOP. It was lunch time and there were only two people in the radio station at the time. Around 12:38 p.m. I received a telephone call on the hotline from the Program Director and morning air-personality Bob Barber. He said, "Check the newswire, someone has shot President Kennedy." I hung up the phone and raced down the hall to the newsroom where I heard bells ringing on the Associated Press teletype machine. I looked at the paper as it printed out:

"FLASH – KENNEDY SHOT IN DALLAS" then **"Here is a Bulletin from the Associated Press."**

"(Dallas, Texas) – President John Kennedy was shot today while in a motorcade in Dallas, Texas." The bulletin went on to say he was rushed to Parkland Hospital at speeds of up to 80 miles per hour.

I ripped the story from the wire and stood at the top of the stairs and yelled down to the one other person in the building at the time: the receptionist, Theresa. I told her to come up stairs as fast as possible and I ran back into the studio and raised the monitor volume of the Mutual Broadcasting Network. I heard soft fill music. I lowered the volume and just as Theresa came into the studio, I ran the production cart of "BULLETIN – BULLETIN – HERE IS A NEWS BULLETIN FROM THE KTOP RADIO NEWSROOM."

It was then I read the bulletin about President Kennedy being shot. While I was re-reading the bulletin and keeping the listeners updated on the situation, I raised the pot (volume of the network channel) on the tall console to my left and I still heard fill music. I lowered the pot (network channel) and went into a commercial. I told Theresa to run back to the AP machine and keep tearing reports off the machine and running them back into the air-studio. I kept monitoring the network and didn't hear any news reports.

Normally our practice was to record the newscast feed at 30 minutes past the hour and play it back at 55 minutes past the hour. Well, I knew the newscast I had just recorded at 12:30 p.m. was outdated so I decided to break format and carry the network when I knew there would be a live newscast at the top of the hour. So I blabbered over and over the same bulletin and all the updates Theresa brought to me. I opened the network pot and at exactly 1 o'clock, Mutual sent down a time tone and their announcer read the updated reports including a live segment from a reporter in Dallas.

We kept the network on the air continuously to just beyond the funeral coverage several days later. This included the live coverage of Lee Harvey Oswald being shot and killed. I was running the board at that moment and about fell out of my chair when I heard the gunfire and the announcer say: **"He's been shot – he's been shot – Lee Oswald has been shot."**

I learned several days later that KTOP was the first radio station to report the assassination of President Kennedy in Topeka and, because it occurred in the lunch hour, a number of newsrooms were empty.

Everyone alive then has a story of where they were when they heard the news that President Kennedy had been killed. That is mine.

In late 1963 a competitor, KJAY radio, changed their call letters to KEWI, played the same Top40 music we did and called themselves: "BIG KEE-WEE." KEWI was 5,000 watts and had a much clearer signal to KTOP's 250-watt sound. K-TOP added some reverb to the signal and announced we were broadcasting from our "new crystal studios." The engineers took an old Wollensak microphone and hooked it up to a separate channel of the main console. The Wollensak's thin, tinny sound made our voices sound like we were coming from a spaceship when we read the weather forecast. We called it: "K-TOP SATELLITE WEATHER" since it was the dawn of the space age and satellites were new to the public. It was all about image. Our regular mic was an Altec Birdcage microphone that produced a fabulous bass sound that made all our voices sound deep and sexy. But KTOP had trouble getting their weak signal over the huge grain elevators along the river. There was no question that KEE-WEE was much stronger than KTOP in sound and coverage. It wasn't long for KEWI to beat us in the ratings.

CHAPTER 3

Where is Sonofabitch?

"Reach Out I'll Be There" – The Four Tops
"Light My Fire" – The Doors
"Mrs. Robinson" – Simon & Garfunkel

I LEFT KTOP IN EARLY 1965 AND WENT TO WORK AT their direct competitor KEWI as News Director. I was already in college at Washburn University and pledged Phi Delta Theta Fraternity. I would work weekday mornings reading news and then go to class in the afternoon and evening. I drove a mobile news car that had a new communication capability. It was a two-way radio, but it was managed by a company with an operator who would connect you to someone via the telephone. The unfortunate thing was everyone who had one of these two-way radios could hear only one side of everyone's conversation. This made it very uncomfortable and sometimes during a live report on the air, another two-way customer would break in asking the operator to dial a different phone number. I would drive the mobile unit on campus at Washburn and it was like a chick-magnet. It had working police and sheriff scanners in the car along with this new mobile telephone two-way. Girls loved to go on dates with me in the mobile unit. We never knew when we'd be out on a date if we would hear on a scanner that there was a news story to cover. It could be a crime scene, an automobile accident or some other emergency. Plus, the mobile unit had a red cherry-top light arrangement on the roof that I could activate whenever I arrived at a news event. I would park next to a police car and we'd all have our emergency red lights flashing. On some evenings I'd take a date for a drive in the country. I'd turn the cherry-top light on when we were on a dark country road. I thought I was a Rock Star!

The radio station was on the top floor of a downtown bank and the studios were very modern for the time. It was at this radio station where I was convinced to change my name. While I was at KTOP I used my legal name. When I joined KEWI the Program Director told me I **had** to change my name. He said my legal name was too associated with KTOP and he wanted me to use something different. I pulled out the Topeka Phone Book and opened it with my eyes closed and pointed to a name on the paper and it was someone named Edwards. I thought of Douglas Edwards of CBS News and I decided I could be Tom Edwards or Tommy Edwards.

I found there was a benefit to having a professional name because I used to get a number of strange phone calls at home during the time I used my legal name. On one occasion a father asked me to talk to his son on the phone about the dangers of alcohol and other times people would call requesting songs or just wanting to talk about the radio station. Having a professional name that was unpublished in the phone book gave me a great deal of privacy. But more importantly it also protected the privacy of my parents and younger brother. I was still new to the business and getting used to the attention.

The war in Vietnam was escalating. Shortly after the Battle of Ia Drang in the fall of 1965, the draft board changed the minimum number of hours for student deferment and I was called in for a physical. I got my 1-A classification and was told I'd probably be drafted into the Army within 60 days. My brother Jack was already in the Navy attending Firefighting School in Philadelphia. I decided I would also join the Navy, so I met with a recruiter who told me I had all the qualifications to be an Air Control Man, now called an Air Traffic Controller. I would probably serve on aircraft carriers or land-based naval air stations. I figured that would be great training so I could have another post military career in case my radio dream fizzled. I signed up, took the oath and was sent to boot camp in late January 1966. Having some college experience, the officers put me in charge of a trainload of new recruits from the Kansas City and Topeka areas on a multi-day trip to San Diego. I had to make sure everyone arrived, and I carried all our personnel records.

After arriving at the Naval Training Center, I had a series of routine medical examinations. Within two weeks I was pulled out of a classroom and told that tests showed I had a collapsed left lung! I was asked if I had trouble breathing and I said I had trouble sleeping because I couldn't get comfortable. I was taken to the Balboa Naval Hospital for treatment. I soon had a tube in my chest and was bedridden for two weeks. Overall, I spent a full month in the hospital and eventually went back to boot camp.

I was placed in a different company of new recruits and I made friends with the Recruit Chief Petty Officer. He was one of us, but he was assigned to be the leader. He was from Hawaii and I wish I could remember his name. A few years later I saw him on TV as a news anchor while I was visiting Hawaii. I recognized him immediately. The real boss of the group was the Company Commander. He was a Chief Petty Officer who already had 20 plus years in the service. He was an old salt and a real hard ass and like all military boot camps, he did his best to break us down and make us perform as a unit with certain disciplines. This guy could never remember my name, so he always called me Sonofabitch. We'd be lined up in formation and he'd yell out, "Where's Sonofabitch?" and I'd run to the front, stand at attention, salute and yell out, "Right here, Sir." This same Company Commander designated me Recruit Educational Petty Officer. A fancy title but all it meant was I was in charge of making sure all the recruits passed the exams because the goal was to win the academic streamer for our company flag.

All the recruits went through everything as a unit. This included firefighting where we actually fought oil fires with choking black smoke inside a concrete building; survival in the water where we would jump in a deep pool, remove our dungaree pants and use them as a temporary life preserver; the firing range where we shot at targets; and surviving chemical and gas attacks where we were ordered to remove our gas masks to experience tear gas. We had many classroom lessons on rules, tradition and the chain of command. It was all preparing us to be sent to the fleet.

The last written exam of boot camp was like a high school final. The Company Commander ordered me to make sure the slowest guys in the company passed the exam even if it took all night before the test. I wound up sitting on the floor next to these guys' bunk beds after lights out going over the study sheets with recruits who had the poorest test scores. I didn't get much sleep, but I knew I'd be in trouble if even one of these fellow recruits failed the test. The fire watch guard would alert me whenever someone was approaching our barracks. I was breaking the rules being out of the rack when not on watch. So, I'd jump in bed and pretend to be asleep. Every other night we all had to serve a one-hour shift as fire guard walking around inside the barracks to keep watch for a fire. Another member had to walk around outside the barracks guarding the laundry on the clothesline. This guard had to carry a rifle and would verbally challenge anyone who approached. We slept better knowing our skivvies were safe from all threats, foreign and domestic!

It all paid off because we won the Academic Streamer for our company flag and when we graduated, the Company Commander called me in and thanked me. And since I was no longer a recruit, his attitude changed 180 degrees and we were both very friendly. He wished me "smooth seas." He was retiring soon, and he hoped I had as much fun as he did in his Navy career. And guess what? He remembered my name!

One of the events during boot camp was to determine what rate I would serve. A rate meant what specialty I was to study in the next school. I was told the rate of Air Control Man was closed and the Navy was going to order me to Communications Yeoman School in Norfolk, Virginia.

My father was the only family member able to attend my graduation from Navy boot camp. My mother had insisted they spend the money to have Dad fly to San Diego for the ceremony. It was the first time I saw a family member after leaving Kansas on a train and spending months in training and weeks in the Naval Hospital from a collapsed lung. I'll never forget seeing him sitting in the bleachers with the other families. There is a point in everyone's life when you realize that your parents are getting older. I had been gone from home for several months and my dad looked like he had aged 10 years. He was in his mid-60s and appeared much older than the last time I saw him.

After graduation from boot camp, I had two weeks of leave to go back home before reporting to school in Norfolk. Just days after I got back to Topeka, a tornado hit the city on June 8, 1966 causing massive destruction. The tornado touched down in the southwest area of Topeka and cut a diagonal path of devastation to the northeast corner of the city. Dad and I were downtown when the tornado sirens began to wail. My car had stalled earlier that day and we were attempting to get it started when we saw the funnel cloud was already on the ground about a mile from our location. It appeared that the tornado was near our house and we both panicked. We jumped in my dad's car and quickly drove away from the danger and took a roundabout way home to find that our house had survived.

The Washburn University campus was hit hard. A huge 300-pound stone from one of the buildings on campus was torn away and thrown two miles. The downtown area was severely damaged, and my car was totaled. Homes were destroyed all along the path of the tornado. Many families lost everything.

Later that day the Program Director at KEWI called and said he had heard I was in town and asked if I would come to the radio station to work. He needed me to be on the air and provide coverage about the tornado. I told him I didn't have a ride back downtown so the Chief Engineer at the station picked me up and drove me to the studios. I worked all night reporting on the damage and injuries. I gathered teletype reports, monitored police scanners and took phone calls from listeners.

My father passed away a week after the tornado of a massive heart attack. The stress was too great. I had to contact the Red Cross and they helped me get an emergency extension to my authorized leave from the Navy. I arranged my Dad's funeral and helped take care of my mom while she tried to cope with losing her husband. By this time, my younger brother Jack was a firefighter in crash crew at Patuxent River Naval Air Station in Maryland. We had to arrange for his trip back to Kansas. My sister JoAnne was living in Topeka with her husband and their children, Cindy and Jim. Our family was close and it was fortunate we could all be there to comfort each other.

Losing my father was heartbreaking.

My relationship with my father wasn't as close as I wanted it to be. He wasn't very supportive of my interest in radio. He never asked me about my job or the people I worked with. I doubt if he knew much about working in radio or TV, so maybe he just didn't 'get it.' But after I joined the Navy and came home on leave, we spent evenings together, and we had wonderful conversations. I remember telling him I loved him just a few evenings before he suffered that heart attack. I had never said that to him before and he had not said it to me. He did say it that evening and it meant so much to me. Since his death there have been many times I have thought about that night and wished that I had told him I loved him more often, but I also feel a sense of comfort knowing that we finally did say those words to each other.

Two weeks after Dad's funeral I hated to leave everyone, but it was time to head east to Norfolk and my new life in the Navy.

The war was raging and there were so many people going through Class A schools in places like Norfolk. These classes involved intense training in a specialized field. There were two shifts per day to attend class: one in the morning and one in the afternoon. I was assigned to a 3 p.m. – 11 p.m. shift. I would get out of class at 11 p.m. and go to the Mess Hall to eat before going to bed. I wouldn't have to be in class the next day until 3 p.m. Since we had mornings off, a friend and I would play handball at the base gym almost every day.

Upon graduation from school, I was ordered to the Naval Station in Washington, DC. From there, I was sent to the Pentagon and placed in what was called a Yeoman's billet handling electronic messages. I was given a Secret security clearance and was told a background check was underway for a Top Secret security clearance. Once the TS clearance was granted, I was ordered into the Assistant Chief of Naval Operations/Communications office and worked directly for Rear Admiral Robert H. Weeks and Captain Robert H. White. I handled very sensitive classified material daily and was eventually given even higher security clearances.

Admiral Weeks eventually retired and Rear Admiral Francis J. Fitzpatrick was my new boss. It was an awesome job working in this office during this time. We had various levels of security and having such a high clearance, I had to be very careful of who saw the material I handled. In some cases, it never left my sight while I had custody of it. For example, on occasion, the Admiral ordered me to carry a document to a particular officer in another area of the Pentagon. I would have to stand off to the side while he or she read it. After they indicated they had read and understood the contents, I would return it to the office or deliver it to a different office to be sent up the chain of command.

It was a very exciting time to be in the Pentagon. While the war in Southeast Asia was still going on, NASA was launching spacecrafts into orbit and eventually to the moon and our office was responsible for providing communications between the recovery ships in the Pacific and the White House. I enjoyed working in this environment, but I missed being on the radio.

My hours in the Pentagon were from 5:45 a.m. – 4:30 p.m. and after a few months, I applied for a job at WEAM radio in Arlington, Virginia. I was first hired as a night newsman and did a newscast every hour from 7 p.m. – midnight. That lasted for several months until the nighttime DJ suddenly left the station and the boss asked me to do the nighttime show. That lasted for the entire duration of my career at WEAM. There are several stories about WEAM 'The Lively One' coming in the next chapter.

The 1967 Middle East War broke out and one of our communication intelligence ships, the USS Liberty, was attacked by the Israelis. Later, The USS Pueblo was pirated by the North Koreans while it was on assignment from the Naval Security Station and from our office to monitor communications. Work had begun on an incredible new antennae installation to communicate with submarines on the bottom of the ocean. It was the early days of satellite communications and the development of ships who could handle large amounts of data. And on top of it all, there was a march on the Pentagon in an anti-war effort with a desire to shut down the military.

First, here is the Pueblo story. I was always the first to arrive in the office in the morning. I would go to the communications shack, a large area across the hall in the C ring and pick up the classified and unclassified messages that came in overnight. I'd fill the coffee thermos and take it back to the office. Then I'd begin to unlock the cabinets containing the classified material. They were combination locks and I had to memorize them all. I'd get the office ready for Captain White who always arrived 15 to 20 minutes after I did. This was usually around 6:00 a.m. As I was arriving at the office one morning, I noticed a young female Ensign standing outside the locked office door. I greeted her, and she asked when the Admiral would arrive that morning. She was the Officer of the Day in the Com-Shack and I said he'd be here around 8:30 but Captain White should be here within 20 minutes. She handed me some colored paper which indicated it was highly classified material. I assured her I'd give it to the Captain as soon as he arrived. I unlocked the door and began unlocking the safes while reading the messages. When I saw the first message that the USS Pueblo had been boarded by North Koreans and she was steaming to a North Korean port, I ran to the phone to call Admiral Fitzpatrick at home. Mrs. Fitzpatrick answered the phone and I asked to speak to him. When he got on the phone I said, "Admiral, you need to get here as soon as possible. Something has happened." He asked, "What happened?" I looked at the subject line of the classified message and the subject was classified so I couldn't tell him on an unsecured phone. I said, "I can't say – subject is classified – but trust me, you need to get here." He hung up and walked into the office about 40 minutes later and we had all the messages spread out on his desk. Captain White saw the messages when he came in and I told him the Admiral was on the way.

As soon as the Admiral arrived at his desk, the direct line from the White House Telecommunications Office rang and he was there to answer it. It was a very exciting day and since all of this hadn't been released to the public that morning, I couldn't say anything to anyone who wasn't authorized at the time.

In October 1967 between 35,000 and 50,000 anti-war demonstrators descended on the Pentagon. Hundreds in the crowd tried to get inside the building. I was ordered to work an overnight shift on the 5th floor E ring, so I had to take the night off at the radio station. All offices had to be left unlocked. I rode what looked like a large tricycle around slowly listening for windows crashing. I had a fire extinguisher to put out any small blaze and then I was to immediately call the security desk. If I saw someone who didn't have authorization to be there, I was to call security and attempt to detain the individual. Fortunately, no windows were broken, no fires broke out and no unauthorized persons showed up in my area. Security personnel walked the halls. I suspected they were also checking to see if I was awake.

I was living in a barracks at Ft. Myer at the time and when the bus drove us to the Pentagon that night around 9 o'clock, huge searchlights on Arlington National Cemetery were shining down on the Pentagon. Soldiers from Ft. Belvoir surrounded the building shoulder-to-shoulder and Marines were camped out on the first floor. Federal Marshals were everywhere and the crowd outside was huge.

We got a short lunch break around 2 o'clock in the morning and some marshals asked if we'd like to go to the roof and see what was happening. A couple of other enlisted guys and I agreed, and we went up to the roof and looked out at the crowds through some night-vision type cameras. All the so-called 'hippies' were relaxing, smoking, building campfires and having parties. I didn't feel there was any imminent threat to the building whatsoever. Plus, it was all for show. There was no way the military would permit the building to be taken over and the most sensitive areas of the Pentagon were guarded by armed soldiers and Marines.

I kept in contact with Admiral Weeks after he retired and after I was discharged. We exchanged letters and Christmas cards for several years. Mary Lou and I were thrilled when the Admiral and Captain White came to our wedding and the reception!

I received an Honorable Discharge from the Navy on Halloween, October 31, 1969.

A couple of other interesting stories happened while I was in the Navy. These stories involved my radio job. One was about a very special girl I met. Another involved two other girls. I think I should describe the latter first.

CHAPTER 4

And They Were Topless!!

"Ain't Nothing Like the Real Thing"
– Marvin Gaye & Tammi Terrell
"Mercy, Mercy, Mercy" – The Buckinghams
"Can't Take My Eyes Off You" – Frankie Valli

IN THE 1960'S, RADIO STATION WEAM 1390 KHZ WAS AN AM radio station licensed to Arlington, Virginia that serviced the Washington, DC metro market. It was a 5,000-watt station formatted to play the top-40 or popular music of the day. The positioning statement was WEAM THE LIVELY ONE. That is how the receptionist always answered the phone. The jocks were collectively known as THE WEAM TEAM RED COATS. We all had to go out and buy a red sports coat for personal appearances and we weren't reimbursed!

Long before computers, it was 45 rpm records on turntables and many live commercials. I was serving in the Navy at the

Pentagon during the day and working at WEAM at night and on the weekends. There are several good radio stories here. Radio people know there are always good radio stories at every radio station.

I first read the news six nights a week. Every hour I read a 5 minute newscast and a longer newscast just before midnight. And I still had to be at the Pentagon no later than 5:45 a.m. the next day.

Some evenings the 7 p.m. – midnight jock on the air would have friends visit him in the studio. This of course, violated station rules, but he didn't care. One evening he had two girls in the studio, and I was in another studio separated by glass. I began reading my news and my peripheral vision caught a lot of movement in the air studio. At the end of a story, I glanced to the adjoining studio and saw that the two girls were dancing in front of the jock.

And they were topless!

He was facing them; they were facing him and me. Obviously, they weren't listening to my newscast and he was playing music on a cue speaker. I was trying to concentrate on reading the news while this was going on in the next studio. Earlier he had told me not to break for a commercial and I could run long if I wanted to. When my newscast was over, I noticed the jock was still facing the dancing girls and was unaware there was dead air. I stood up and started waving my arms frantically trying to get his attention. The girls waved back at me while they were still dancing. Finally, I ran down the hall to the air studio and told him there was dead air. He turned around and played something on a cart and went back to his show. The girls stayed with him for about an hour – still topless. He either sounded distracted or didn't talk at all – just segued the music and the jiggled – uh I mean the jingles. The girls finally left, and he returned to doing the show.

One night about a week later, he didn't show up for work. The afternoon jock stayed on the air thinking he was just running late. He never showed up. After about 45 minutes the program director called and asked me what was happening. I told him the jock hadn't shown up, so he told me I was to do the show that night. I was called the next day while working in the Pentagon and was told the show was now mine. I ended up doing the show daily for a couple of years.

In 2016, I reconnected with that jock on Facebook when he sent me a friend request. I asked him if he was the same jock who once worked at WEAM. He responded, "How did you know that?" I told him I was the guy reading news while he was there and once he left, I took over the night show. He responded, "I didn't leave, I got thrown out."

WEAM is where I first met Al Brady Law. Al and I would work together again in New York City at WOR-FM. At WEAM, Al used the name Happy O'Hare. I have no idea why he used a stupid name like that but WEAM made several people use their standard station names. At WEAM if you did afternoons your on-air name was Russ Wheeler. Another standard station name for the overnight jock was Lee Dawn. When I was doing the 7 p.m.– midnight show, I would go into the production studio after I finished my show and record voice-tracks saying my name was Lee Dawn. Those tracks would run during the automated all night show. Let's not forget I needed to be at the Pentagon a few hours later. Eventually, the standard names were phased out. New air talent could use their real or professional names and weren't required to use one of the names associated with the shift they performed.

I can remember some funny stories about this station including one that involved a guy who sent an air-check to the program director looking for a job. An air-check is an abbreviated tape of the DJ's voice and production with the majority of the songs edited down. The PD hired him for the afternoon drive show based on the air-check alone. As a matter of fact, the PD played the air-check for the rest of us a few days before the talent arrived at the station and we were all very impressed.

The day the new guy started for his PM Drive shift, I got out of the office at the Pentagon and jumped into my MGB sports car, turned on the radio and I couldn't believe my ears. The guy was terrible! He sounded as though he had never done a radio show in his life. He didn't know what to say and he had no idea how to run a format. There were long pauses between the songs and commercials. Something wasn't right. He didn't sound anything like his air-check. His voice was completely different from what I remembered hearing on the tape. I couldn't wait to get to the radio station and find out what was happening.

When I arrived at the station, I went into the air studio to meet him. There was copy paper, newspapers, cups and trash everywhere. The Program Log was a mess, as it was obvious he hadn't signed on and there were required entries missing from it. And the 45 rpm records were scattered everywhere. They were on the console, on the floor and a spare turntable. I commented, "You don't sound like your air-check," and he replied, "Oh, that wasn't me. It was a friend's air-check. I knew I'd never get hired if I sent one of my air-checks." I didn't get the chance to ask the PD about him. He was gone the next day. The PD left shortly after that.

I thought we were ALL GONE one day in 1968. The General Manager of WEAM was a bit odd. He had several rules that I thought were petty, but they weren't unreasonable. One day his secretary called me while I was working at the Pentagon to tell me the entire air staff had been fired! I said, "What? I've been fired? We've all been fired?" She said yes and all of the other jocks had been called into his office but since I was working at the Pentagon, she decided to call me. She added that he wanted to talk to me, so I waited for him to come on the line. When I heard his voice he said, "Hi Tommy. I've fired everyone but I'm rehiring you. So, you're on the air tonight." I said OK and we hung up. I found out later he rehired everyone that afternoon. I don't remember why we were all fired but honestly, it didn't surprise any of us. Like I said, he was a bit odd!

Some talented guys came through WEAM in their careers. That includes Richie Sher. Richie was from Baltimore and I thought he sounded terrific. He had a great voice and compelling content in what he said on the air. He knew the music and more importantly, he knew the audience that was listening. Richie returned to Baltimore and had success in radio and TV. He eventually co-hosted a television show with Oprah Winfrey.

There were other great voices at WEAM, including news people. One name and one voice I remember was Dave Humphrey. His voice was authoritative, believable yet not condescending. Since my first job at WEAM was as a newsperson, I considered Humphrey a leader and someone I wanted to learn from.

I saw something while working at WEAM that I had heard about in my career but had never witnessed before. It was a broadcast of a baseball game being recreated in a radio studio. Instead of the announcer being at the ballpark, he was in the WEAM news-room reading the events of a Baltimore Orioles game from a ticker tape type device. He did play by play of the game while sitting in the studio. He used sound effects of a crowd that was always in the background and he tapped his pencil on a wooden block to make the sound of a bat hitting a ball. All the while he ad-libbed about what kind of day it was, stories about the players, description of the weather and other things without actually watching any of the game. He added his own live commercials between innings. He was there only once, and it was fascinating to watch him work.

Over time WEAM 1390 kHz has evolved to different call letters and different formats. As of this writing, the station is known as WZHF. It simulcasts the English language Radio Sputnik Network full time. According to Wikipedia, WZHF is registered as an agent of the Russian government.

I had a lot of fun working at WEAM. From topless women, to a phony jock, to being fired and rehired the same day, to watching a guy recreate a baseball game in the studio, I saw it all. And during all this, I was experiencing all the excitement of working in the Pentagon. But there was something even more exciting during that time… it was where I met and fell in love with Mary Lou.

CHAPTER 5

Hello Mary Lou

"You Are So Beautiful" – Joe Cocker
"The Look of Love" – Dusty Springfield
"Too Busy Thinking About My Baby" – Marvin Gaye

RADIO STATION WEAM WAS LOCATED IN SUBURBAN Arlington, Virginia in a residential neighborhood. The station was actually inside a building designed to look like a big colonial house with a large field out back that held the tower structure. An asphalt parking lot was also built into the back yard. The front door and the broadcast operations were located on the ground floor. The sales department, management, public affairs, and finance departments were located on the second floor. The receptionist sat at a desk on the second level in a position to be able to view and greet visitors entering the front door. Just inside the front door, there was an electronic door to the on-air operations center where the studios and programming offices were located. There was also a staircase to the upper level. The receptionist would have to remotely unlock the door when staff members needed access to the studios. There was a basement in the building, but it was primarily used for storage. However, there was also a large, very comfortable overstuffed chair down there. Since my days at the Pentagon were long, I would sometimes sit in that chair and take a 20-minute nap before I went on the air. It was surprising how refreshing that short snooze would be.

I rarely had any business upstairs and normally I would enter the building through the back door which was in an area where the transmitter equipment was located. But one day early in 1968 I had the afternoon off at the Pentagon and went to the radio station for a meeting. I entered through the front door and without paying much attention to the receptionist, I tried to open the electronic door but I wasn't given access. I stepped back and looked up at the new receptionist on the second floor. She was a beautiful blonde and I said, "Are you going to let me in or what?" She said, "Well, who are you?" I said, "I'm Tommy Edwards – buzz me through." I guess I came off rather arrogant because she gave me a look and said, "Well, isn't that a big deal!" She unlocked the door and I went into a production studio and asked one of the jocks, "Who's the cute blonde upstairs with the attitude?" He told me that it was Mary Lou, the new receptionist. She had started working at WEAM a few weeks before and we had spoken on the phone a few times. I would call the station just to check in and we would usually laugh about something that was happening or a silly memo from the General Manager that she had put in my mailbox. I had been looking forward to meeting her. I felt bad about our first face-to-face encounter, so I needed to apologize. Eventually, I went upstairs and introduced myself a second time. This time I was greeted with a big smile. She forgave me for being rude and we ended up laughing about the experience. I continued to call the station several times a week – sometimes just to talk to her. I wanted to check on whatever was happening at the station and she'd call me with things I needed to know regarding contests and promotions. We would talk about subjects other than the radio station and over time I learned she had a boyfriend and I told her about my girlfriend.

It wasn't long until Mary Lou invited me and my girlfriend to parties at her apartment. She shared the apartment with a friend named Pat who worked at the Central Intelligence Agency and I learned later that Mary Lou had applied for a job there too. Unlike other broadcast facilities, WEAM advertised their job openings at the radio station over the air, including the receptionist position. Mary Lou heard it while listening in her car one day. She decided to apply to make some money until the CIA security clearance background check was complete. She went to the station the next day and was hired almost immediately. When the job at the Agency did become available, she turned it down to stay at the radio station. And I'm so glad she did.

Along with being the receptionist, Mary Lou also worked for Music Director, Paul Christy, and for Program Director/Morning Show Host, Lee Stevens. Stevens would later be replaced as PD by Ted Clarke. She would screen calls from record company representatives and type up weekly survey information. Mary Lou and Sandy Burke, the Promotion Director, would be sent out with the jocks on personal appearances.

Representatives from record companies made weekly visits to the radio station to promote new releases. They always met with the Music Director but first spent some time talking to Mary Lou. One day a record guy walked in the front door with Ricky Nelson. She spotted Ricky immediately and stood up. He walked up the stairs and approached her desk, took her hand, looked her right in the eye and said, "Hello, Mary Lou." She was so excited she called me at the Pentagon. I told her, "He should have sung it."

Several months went by and we became very good friends. One Saturday evening in late September, a mutual friend Paul Clarke and I were working the night shift at WEAM. Paul was a newsman and I was the jock on the air. Before our shift started, we were hanging out in the production studio. Mary Lou had stopped by the radio station to pick up some materials for a special project she was working on for the General Sales Manager and came into the studio to say hi. We told her we were going to Georgetown after we got off the air at midnight and asked if she wanted to meet and go with us. She said, "Let me call Sandy and see if she wants to come along." Mary Lou called us later and said she and Sandy would meet us at the radio station at midnight. When we got off the air, Paul drove the four of us to a tavern called The Brickskeller. Once we were there, we ordered a couple of pitchers of beer and we had a great time. We already knew each other, and the experience was more exciting because we were now getting to know each other in a more social/fun and even romantic setting.

We returned later to the radio station's parking lot and went our separate ways.

I remember all four of us had to attend a football game that was part of a promotion for the radio station the next morning.

We couldn't let on that we had all just been out together almost all night, but we made the appearance and then went out for breakfast.

That experience was the beginning of us falling in love. I loved being with her and it was so easy to talk to her about anything. We were very comfortable together and I told her I was going to break up with my girlfriend which I did a day or two later. Mary Lou broke up with her boyfriend several days later and we became a close-knit couple.

The radio station had a policy of no dating between employees and we thought we would have to keep it a big secret. But Mary Lou eventually told Margaret, the General Manager's Secretary, who talked to the GM and got his approval. Our secret was out.

Our relationship was exciting and a little unique. We worked together at the same radio station but not during the same hours. Mary Lou worked during normal business hours and I would arrive around 6 p.m., go on the air at 7 p.m. and get off the air at midnight. So, we didn't see each other much except on the weekends.

I remember one day I was asked to work the midday shift on the air. I was able to take the day off at the Pentagon. Mary Lou stopped by the studio and offered to go out and buy lunch. When she returned to the station and as she entered the studio, I was playing "The Look of Love." She said, "I love this song" and placed my lunch on the turntable that was on the air at that moment. The arm and needle scraped across the record as I scrambled to turn on the mic and back announced the song saying "That's Jackie DeShannon." Mary Lou was horrified that she had caused this problem but not enough to keep her from saying, "No it's not

– that's Dusty Springfield." Of course, all of this was on the air! I stumbled around to get a new record on the air and then asked her to leave the studio but leave the lunch. That crazy scene has been a source of laughter all these years when we talk about it. Sometimes she says that I married her to keep her out of the studio.

Mary Lou and I had a short courtship. I knew she was the girl for me, and I asked her to marry me on New Year's Eve. We were married in June of 1969. It was a beautiful day in Northern Virginia. Several of my family members and a fraternity brother came in from Kansas. Members of Mary Lou's family from Maryland, Massachusetts and New Jersey were there. Of course, we included Paul Clarke and Sandy Burke in our wedding party. Years later Mary Lou told me that just as she was ready to walk down the aisle, she was so nervous she looked at her dad and said, "I can't do this." Her father laughed and gave her a nudge and said, "You *have* to do this. Everything is paid for." She said she laughed and told me when she saw the smile on my face, she knew everything was going to be all right. Our first dance at the reception as husband and wife was to what else? "The Look of Love" by Dusty Springfield.

We honeymooned in St. Croix, U.S. Virgin Islands at a small hotel on the beach. There were many newlyweds at the hotel and we just naturally enjoyed hanging with everyone at cocktail time. Neither one of us had ever been to the Caribbean. After traveling all day, we arrived at the hotel a little tired and very hungry. We were told by the front desk that dinner wouldn't be served for more than an hour. When we asked if there was somewhere in the hotel where we could get a bottle of water and maybe a bag of chips, we were informed with a very serious tone that "We don't have *chips* in the islands!" Oops!!

When we returned to the Washington, DC area, we got an apartment in Falls Church, VA. Our plan at that time was to continue working at the radio station and wait until I was discharged from the Navy to decide where we would live.

One of the frequent callers to the radio station was Bob Hamilton, a Los Angeles based editor for a weekly radio tip-sheet. His report featured radio rumors and reports of what radio stations were playing what songs. It was a highly respected weekly publication. Mary Lou would talk to Bob regularly and during one conversation she mentioned that she and I were newly married, and he asked her for an air-check of my show. I mailed an air-check to him just in time for him to toss it into his suitcase because he was heading to New York City.

Once he was in New York he gave the air-check to Sebastian Stone, the Program Director at WOR-FM, to review. It was that air-check delivered by Bob Hamilton that triggered a phone call from Sebastian to WEAM Radio looking to invite me to New York for an interview. Mary Lou took the call and contacted me at the Pentagon with the exciting news. I called Sebastian from a pay phone on the Pentagon Rotunda and set up a trip to New York to meet with him. That led to an incredible job opportunity in New York City.

CHAPTER 6

The City that Never Sleeps

"I Can't Get Next to You" – The Temptations
"Something" – The Beatles
"Crystal Blue Persuasion" – Tommy James & The Shondells

IN THE MEETING WITH SEBASTIAN AND GENERAL Manager Ron Ruth, I was offered two weekend shifts on WOR-FM, (known in the industry as "OR-FM"), and an eventual full-time gig when I got out of the Navy. My shifts on the weekend were midnight to 6 a.m. on Saturday and 9 a.m. – 3 p.m. on Sunday. I learned I would make more money in those two days per week than I did working 6 days a week at WEAM. I couldn't believe it.

In my original phone call with Sebastian, I was asked for my birth date. I didn't think much of it at the time but later I learned that Sebastian's wife Pat was very much into astrology and she eventually compiled my astrological chart. Sebastian told me in my meeting with him and Ron Ruth that my "Venus was rising." I guess that was a good sign. I didn't know it was that obvious!

From then on, I would fly to New York in my Navy uniform on the Eastern Shuttle for a cheap military fare every Friday afternoon and check into the Biltmore Hotel still in uniform. I'd get a military rate there, too. I would change clothes and walk to the radio station for weekly meetings with the rest of the air staff. After almost every meeting we would all stop by Child's Restaurant on the first floor of the 1440 Broadway building for a cocktail. Sebastian would come down around 6 p.m. and have a drink with us and pick up the tab. I'd head back to the hotel to take a nap before I went on the air at midnight.

After I got off the air Saturday morning, I'd head back to the hotel to sleep. In the meantime, Mary Lou would catch the shuttle to New York and arrive at the hotel. She'd quietly drop off her overnight bag in the room and head out shopping and sightseeing until about 3 p.m. By the time she got back, I'd be ready to join her. We'd go out and take long walks and explore the city then have a nice dinner at an inexpensive restaurant. We'd catch a movie before going back to the hotel. I'd get up early Sunday morning and do the 9 a.m. – 3 p.m. show. Mary Lou would then meet me, and we'd catch a cab to LaGuardia Airport. We would fly back on the shuttle to Washington, DC after an exciting and fun weekend in New York City.

In 1969 President Richard Nixon announced that some military people would be discharged early to save money. My original discharge date was in the first quarter of 1970, but word came down that I would be given an Honorable Discharge on October 31st, 1969. I notified Sebastian of this change and he told me since I was being discharged on Friday, October 31st, I'd start my full-time Noon to 3 p.m. shift the following Monday.

We had just enough time to plan our move from Virginia to New York City. While I went through the final days of military service, Mary Lou flew to New York to supervise our furniture's arrival. We had found an apartment on East 77th Street on the Upper East Side of Manhattan. It was located on the 31st floor overlooking the East River and Queens. John Jay Park was next to the building and kids were always playing basketball there.

I joined Mary Lou in the city the evening of October 31st. We soon began exploring our neighborhood. We were newly married, and we enjoyed our ability to go anywhere at any time for movies, concerts, dinner and sightseeing. We sold our cars before we left Virginia. While we lived in New York we either walked, took the subway or hailed a cab. The subway was a real bargain at that time. It was only 20 cents per person per ride.

We spent many afternoons in Central Park. We loved walking around Rockefeller Center and the United Nations area. We particularly enjoyed taking the Circle Line boat ride around Manhattan and riding the Staten Island Ferry. We fell in love with New York.

WOR-FM was truly a great radio station. Sebastian Stone was very influential in my career in giving me good direction and displaying a strong work ethic. He was a great leader who insisted on perfection. He made me feel welcome and immediately treated me like an important part of the team.

He would wake up late at night and call the hotline just to let the jock on the air know he was listening. This happened to me when I was part-time on the overnight show. I was shocked when the hotline lit-up and all he said was, "Hey man, you sound down.

Everything ok?" I'd say, "YES! I feel great." And he'd say, "Then let me hear it." And he would hang up.

New York is the city that never sleeps, and the listening was huge any time of the day. We even had girls who worked shifts answering the request lines 7 days a week! There were small telephone lights on the wall that were constantly blinking. One row of lights was for Manhattan and The Bronx. There was another for Brooklyn, Queens and Long Island. The third was for Staten Island and yet another row was for New Jersey. The hotline was a red light at eye level in front of the DJ. It also was equipped to blink twice as fast as the other phone lights and had the word **tilt** on it. When the hotline rang, the jock was to answer it as fast as possible with "Hotline." It was always Sebastian calling with an observation he wanted us to work on.

WOR-FM was beginning to put pressure on longtime ratings king WABC-AM. I had only been with the station a few months when Rick Sklar, the Program Director of WABC called while I was on the air. He asked me to meet him at a bar a block from his office on 6th Avenue. It was here he asked me to audition for the overnight show on WABC by reading some of the sponsor's commercials for *Dennison Men's Clothing* in Union, New Jersey. I agreed. We went to the WABC studios where I recorded a few live commercials. The next day I told Sebastian and Ron about the offer and they simply said, "You can't leave." I had not signed any contract, so I said, "Huh?" And they repeated, "You can't leave and that's that." Talk about being a gullible inexperienced guy now living in New York! I said, "OK" and I called Sklar and told him I was staying at OR-FM.

The station was owned by RKO General, a division of General Tire. OR-FM was following the Bill Drake Format that he developed. There was no one in the radio business more powerful at that time than Drake. He was responsible for hugely popular and successful radio stations in Los Angeles, Detroit/Windsor, San Francisco, Boston and New York. Drake was someone I wanted to meet sometime but I doubted it would ever happen.

Most radio stations at the time had a "listen line." It was a special phone number executives could call from any city and listen to a particular radio station on the telephone. Those phone numbers were usually very secret so that whenever a broadcast executive wanted to listen to a station across the country, the line would usually be available. WOR-FM had such a line and early one day during my full-time show, the hotline started blinking.

I answered it, "Hotline" and the voice said, "Hello, Tommy? This is Bill Drake."

No way he'd be calling me so it must be a prank.

I said, "Oh yeah? I don't believe you," and I hung up.

A few minutes later during a song, Sebastian kicked the studio door open with fire in his eyes and said, "You idiot! You hung up on Bill Drake!"

I know my face must have shown that I was in complete shock. "What? I didn't think it was him."

Sebastian said, "Why did you hang up on Bill Drake?"

I said, "Why would he be calling me?"

"I don't know," Sebastian said. "You need to call him as soon as you're off the air and apologize." I assured him I would.

I was scared to death. I was worried this dream job was going to end before Christmas. I called Drake after I got off the air from a quiet studio and he laughed and said no one had ever hung up on him before. I apologized over and over. He said he just called to say he was enjoying listening to me on the listen line. I thanked him and he said, "Don't worry. I know we'll get together next time I'm in New York."

We had so many opportunities to meet recording artists and producers while living in New York. Phil Spector called me several times while I was on the air at OR-FM usually after I played one of the hit songs he produced. There were so many of his songs on the WOR-FM playlist. They included songs by The Ronettes, The Crystals, Darlene Love, John Lennon, The Righteous Brothers and many more. When *The Concert for Bangladesh* film was premiering in New York City, Spector requested we finally meet in person in the lobby of the theatre. He helped to produce the concert and I wanted to finally meet the genius face to face. We would meet again years later at a Rock n Roll Hall of Fame event in Los Angeles.

Carly Simon asked a few of us to listen to her first album and give her feedback on what we thought should be her first single. We all agreed on the song "That's the Way I've Always Heard It Should Be." She released it in 1971. We did a concert for wounded servicemen at a local VA Hospital and I introduced Don McLean to the crowd. At that time he was just beginning to make a name in the business. A few weeks later OR-FM began playing his first hit, "American Pie." He had performed the song at the concert, and when I heard it, I knew he was going to be a star. It was a special night with just Don and his acoustic guitar. I felt he made a connection with the wounded warriors. I also had the opportunity to introduce The Bee Gees and The Fifth Dimension at Lincoln Center.

WOR-FM had a public affairs program where we interviewed city officials and celebrities. I conducted several of these interviews including *The Happy Hooker*, Xaviera Hollander. I mentioned after the interview her description in the book of where she lived made me think it was where my wife and I were living. She confirmed it was. When I told Mary Lou about it that evening, she laughed and said, "Maybe we'll bump into her in the lobby."

When I interviewed Jimmy Webb, he told me that after he wrote "McArthur Park" he wanted The Association to record it. They turned him down. Actor Richard Harris eventually provided the vocal track to the song. Webb also wrote such great songs as "By the Time I Get to Phoenix" and "Wichita Lineman."

One exciting thing Mary Lou and I got to experience was when record companies invited us and the other jocks to places like the Waldorf Astoria Hotel's Empire Room to have dinner and see famous acts such as Johnny Mathis. Following his performance, we were invited to his suite at the hotel and we had a chance to chat with Johnny and see a painting he was working on.

We enjoyed watching Gladys Knight & the Pips at the Royal Box at the Lowes Americana Hotel.

We spent many evenings at the legendary Copacabana night club on East 60th street. Most of the big names appeared there. We had the chance to enjoy The Supremes, The Temptations, Martha & The Vandellas, Bobby Darin and Tom Jones. When Tom Jones performed there, the crowd outside the club was so huge, we were ushered in through the kitchen entrance. We can confirm the reports of women throwing hotel keys and underwear at him during his show. Bodyguards cradled his head when he came out through the crowd because we learned later, women would try to grab his hair for a souvenir.

The bar at the Copa was at street level and the dining area where the shows were performed was downstairs. Tables were jammed in and new tables would be added in the front row if a special celebrity couple arrived just before the show. No one cared about it being crowded. It was always a special night and it was a great time to live in that great city!

Madison Square Garden was the place to see Elvis Presley, George Harrison's Concert for Bangladesh and Oldies Concerts promoted by Richard Nader. One Oldies Concert I'll never forget featured Ricky Nelson. Ricky came to WOR-FM a day before his concert and I had the opportunity to meet and talk with him. At the concert the next night, Nelson came out on stage and instead of doing some of his hits from the '50s and '60s, he did "Honkey-Tonk Women" and songs by other artists and was eventually booed off the stage. Ricky later went on to write and record a song about that experience called "Garden Party."

Carnegie Hall is where we loved seeing Neil Diamond, Chicago and Crosby, Stills, Nash & Young. I remember that CSN&Y concert because the guys forgot some of the words to "Suite: Judy Blue Eyes." The audience started singing the line and they said "Oh, right" and picked up where the audience left off. We saw Van Morrison at Fillmore East.

There were very talented jocks at OR-FM that I admired and became close friends with. Johnny Donovan, Al Brady and Sean Casey were there when I arrived. Bob Evans, whose real name is Jim Davis and Walt "Baby" Love had come from CKLW in Detroit/Windsor. Joe McCoy was working weekends and we also became friends. After I left OR-FM for WLS in Chicago, Joe took over the midday shift full time. He later became the legendary Program Director of WCBS-FM in New York.

Every once in a while, Mary Lou and I would rent a car for the day to leave the city and drive into areas of New York State not far from the Big Apple. One Saturday we invited Al Brady and his wife Chris to join us. Al and Chris lived just across the Hudson in New Jersey. We picked them up at Port Authority and drove up through White Plains and Tarrytown, New York. We always enjoyed getting out of the city for a day. It was during that afternoon, we stopped at an antique store and I found a Thomas Edison cylinder phonograph. I can't recall how much it cost but it was reasonable, and I came very close to buying it. The phonograph was in working condition and it came with a couple of cylinder recordings. I've always regretted not getting it.

One of the things we always did on these car trips is stop at a suburban grocery store to buy Heinz 57 Steak Sauce and some Dr. Pepper soft drinks. They were nowhere to be found in Manhattan grocery stores back in 1969 and 1970. And McDonald's wasn't in Manhattan back in those days. We'd always treat ourselves to Big Macs. You might think that's silly, but it was special to us back in those days.

Johnny Donovan introduced us to The Downbeat, one of the great jazz clubs in the city. We loved going there and it became a regular spot to take friends visiting from out of town. It was a terrific place to experience New York City nightlife.

One day we were shopping at Gimbels Department Store and we walked through the pet department and saw a Yorkshire Terrier puppy we just had to have. We named her Aphrodite and we took her back to our tiny apartment. House training was a nightmare sometimes, but we loved taking her for walks around our neighborhood.

WOR-FM was a union shop which meant I had to join The American Federation of Television and Radio Artists (AFTRA). I didn't understand then how important belonging to that union would be throughout my whole career. At OR-FM it meant there was a good starting salary that provided Mary Lou and me with very nice living conditions and a chance to travel. Having time to travel was also a part of the agreement with the radio station and AFTRA. The good news? I was eligible for 3 weeks of vacation every year. However, I had to take all of my vacation days at one time between late May and the middle of September. Only one member of the air-staff could be on vacation at a time. That was Sebastian's rule. We took multiple trips during those 3 weeks to see our families and still had time for a private getaway. Once vacation was over, it was like starting fresh all over again. Mary Lou was working a normal 9 a.m. – 5 p.m. job for "The Bob Hamilton Radio Report." Later she joined *Teen Magazine* as Assistant Beauty Editor. In both cases, she was fortunate to be able to take 3 weeks off for our trips.

Since my show was only 3 hours a day Monday – Friday, if there was no production to voice or interviews to conduct, I'd occasionally take off and explore different areas of Manhattan that I had not seen before. One day I took the subway uptown to Harlem.

I always heard about The Apollo Theater on 125th street. It was the place where so many great acts got their big break and those acts would return for shows long after they became stars. I got on the subway and headed north and got off at the 125th Street Station. I found the Apollo Theatre and walked a few blocks in different directions and eventually someone stopped me and asked what I was doing. I said I just moved to New York and always heard about the Apollo Theatre and wanted to see it for myself.

The late 60s and early 70s were intense in New York City. There was so much political unrest. Times were changing. There were anti-war demonstrators in the streets. Some were marked with violence due to the demonstrators being hassled by construction workers. The women's liberation movement was very active. There were impassioned demonstrations demanding equality. Uninhibited demonstrators were burning their bras in bonfires. The Woodstock Music Festival in August of '69 turned out to be one of the most historic and significant cultural events in history. Young people were celebrating new freedoms of expression in their music, in their dress and in their behavior. America was changing, and we witnessed all of this in the streets of New York.

Sebastian Stone eventually left WOR-FM for San Francisco. Mel Phillips moved from WRKO in Boston to WOR-FM as the new Program Director after having great success in Boston.

I was very interested in becoming a program director myself and eventually, Bill Drake came to New York, so I asked for a meeting. We had a late lunch off Park Avenue. During lunch, I asked for the PD job at WRKO, vacated by Phillips. When it was given to someone else, I realized I'd have to wait.

Mary Lou became pregnant in late 1971 while we were living in New York and we thought we would be raising our child in the city but that was not meant to be.

In April 1972 I was contacted by Mike McCormick, Program Director at WLS Radio in Chicago who asked if I'd be interested in considering a move to the Windy City. He offered me the position of Assistant Program Director/Production Director. This was a gig I felt I was ready for.

Living and working in New York City was truly a wonderful experience. The city can be so intimidating at first. But thanks to the most influential program director I've ever worked for it was truly exciting.

CHAPTER 7

WLS

"Crocodile Rock" – Elton John
"Long Cool Woman" – The Hollies
"Feelin' Stronger Everyday" – Chicago

The Rock of Chicago

SINCE WOR-FM HAD BEEN HURTING THE DOMINATING WABC in the ratings, it was obvious that Rick Sklar had to do something. He needed to slow the momentum OR-FM was building. When I met with Rick, I told him I wanted to be a program director someday. I assumed that's what initiated a call from Mike McCormick, the Program Director of ABC Owned WLS in Chicago.

I flew to Chicago at the invitation of McCormick and met with him and General Manager Paul Abrams at the radio station studios.

Later that day I went to dinner with McCormick and his wife at a restaurant in Arlington Heights. That's when he offered me the job of being Assistant Program Director/Production Director with his plan of advancing to General Manager. He told me that after he was named GM, I would be promoted to Program Director. I told him I wanted to talk it over with Mary Lou who was pregnant with our first child. I returned to New York and we decided that although the timing could be better, it was the right thing for us. I resigned from WOR-FM and we were off to The Windy City.

We moved to Chicago in June 1972 about 6 weeks before our daughter Shannon was born, and our life changed. We had a new job in a new city and now a beautiful new baby.

My first day at WLS was June 12, 1972. It was my second day there that I met the legendary Larry Lujack. Larry had recently resigned from WLS and was about to go to our chief competitor WCFL to do afternoon drive. Larry was still on the air at WLS. I went up to him in the studio and offered my hand when I introduced myself. I said, "I'm Tommy Edwards, Larry." He said, "I don't shake hands with people from New York," and he walked away. Larry would later deny that ever happened and I said to him that it was such a shock to me I could never forget it. I didn't like him then, but my opinion changed about a year later during a phone call I received from him while he was at WCFL. It was my first clue there was another side of Lujack.

Mike McCormick had already hired Charlie Van Dyke from Los Angeles to replace Lujack. Charlie has a strong and distinctive voice and is very creative. He is a team player. Once Larry worked through the end of his agreement, Charlie arrived to take over the morning show. I was still new to the station but was asked to sit in the studio with Charlie his first day on-the-air. During the time Charlie was at WLS, he came up with several terrific ideas for promotions and public service events.

It was only a couple of months after I arrived in Chicago that WOR-FM General Manager Ron Ruth asked me to fly back to New York for a quick meeting at LaGuardia Airport. I took a flight on a Saturday morning and met with Ron and General Sales Manager Goff Lebarr in a lounge at the airport. They worked on convincing me that I should forget Chicago and come back to New York and program WOR-FM as it was changing its call letters to WXLO and adjusting its format. I flew back to Chicago that day and Mary Lou and I used that weekend to discuss our options.

We loved living in New York City and the offer they made was most attractive. However, our first child Shannon had been born just a few weeks earlier and moving again would be quite a challenge. We lived in an apartment in the northwest suburbs. Mary Lou and I talked about it for hours and we decided I should go in and see Abrams and McCormick and tell them about the offer. They made a counteroffer and that made our decision to stay in Chicago even easier. I often wonder what would have happened if we had returned to NYC. We enjoyed our time there. But as it turned out, Chicago was very rewarding, and we called it home for a long time.

Unions in Chicago were very powerful and that was a fact of life at WLS. Jocks were all members of one union, AFTRA, and when they were on the air, they weren't permitted to turn their microphones on and off. They had to flash hand signals to a board operator that belonged to a different union: The International Brotherhood of Electrical Workers. Jocks weren't permitted to adjust the volume of their headphones nor the volume of the studio monitor. The microphone would be placed in cue when it wasn't on-the-air so the jock could verbally request for the board operator to raise or lower the volume and ask for the next jingle and song to be loaded in the cart machine. They did have one lever that would mute the microphone temporarily. They'd use it as a cough switch. That would also mute private conversations on the phone and in the studio.

The music we played on the air was on carts. The audio had to be transferred from records and that involved yet another union: The American Federation of Musicians. Only those union members could put the arm of the turntable on a record before the audio could be recorded on tape. That included music and sound effects on discs. Once it was on magnetic tape, it would be under the jurisdiction of the board operator union mentioned earlier. Those members were also the only ones to have jurisdiction over tape machines and the editing of recording tape. The maintenance of the transmitter and news writers were under the jurisdiction of a fourth union: The National Association of Broadcast Employees and Technicians.

When I was Production Director, I had the authorization to play records on a turntable in my office to audition production music. The Music Director and Program Director were also permitted to use a record player to listen to new music in their offices.

I would be remiss if I didn't mention the two gentlemen who were members of the musician's union. First, there was Karl Davis whose nickname was "Colonel" who worked half days in the morning. Karl was an Honorary Kentucky Colonel awarded by the State of Kentucky Legislature for composing the classic song

"Kentucky." Ed Muzard – with the nickname "Moose"- worked afternoons. These two wonderful men were holdovers from the live musicians who performed on *The National Barn Dance* back in the early days of WLS. They were always cheerful and cooperative. Everyone loved "The Colonel" and "Moose."

One might think it would be very difficult and confusing to be able to produce creative promos and commercials while respecting each union member's job. It was a challenge but also a team effort and it never interfered with us doing our best work.

Two things concerned me when I first arrived at WLS. First, the vibe around the radio station seemed strange. An example of that was a phone call Mary Lou received at home during the day asking about my position at WLS and specifically what my salary was. She wasn't comfortable with how they identified themselves or the questions they asked so she refused to speak to them and hung up. The second thing that concerned me was I could sense the tension between Program Director Mike McCormick and General Manager Paul Abrams.

Mike McCormick was a big man, at least 6 foot 6 inches tall. Paul Abrams was short and both men were balding. Mike had told me in the interview that he was going to be named General Manager of WLS after Paul was transferred back to New York. Paul had been a sales executive at WABC in New York before he was transferred to WLS. I assumed this was already set up because of the conversation we had at our first dinner. It was obvious it was going to be complicated. I sensed a power war between these two men and Abrams wasn't about to give in. These guys didn't like each other. They shared a secretary who witnessed the competition daily. McCormick was a World War II buff and he had a toy tank on his desk that he would point out to whoever was sitting in the guest chair. He desperately wanted to be a General Manager. Abrams asked people to spend time in his office in casual conversation. He wanted to be liked and appeared to be insecure at times.

Soon after I arrived, McCormick and I traveled to Dallas to cut new jingles for the radio station. Since WLS could be heard at night in Dallas, McCormick would tune-in briefly and would then call the air studio's hotline to complain about something he heard just to let the talent know he was listening. I think he enjoyed intimidating the air-talent.

Mike would criticize Paul every chance he got. I figured this situation wouldn't last long. But it did last almost a year. Finally, in the spring of 1973, one year after I arrived at WLS, Abrams fired McCormick. I was named Program Director on that same day. I remember that day and where I was when I was told I had a new job. It didn't happen in my office or Paul Abrams' office. It was not in a hallway or a studio. I was in the men's room at the radio station when Abrams walked in and told me I was now the Program Director. By the way, I can remember exactly what I was doing when Abrams walked in. Don't worry. I'm not going to go into that. I decided it wasn't a good time to shake his hand.

Mike went on to be General Manager of a station in Indianapolis called Windy in Indy – WNDE. He hired Jim Davis, who was the program director of the FM station at WLS – called WDAI – as program director for WNDE. Jim was another talent from WOR-FM in New York I worked with that ABC spirited away.

As Program Director I knew we needed to make some changes at WLS and I had written a proposal outlining ideas for on-air talent, new station promotion liners, new on-air positioning statements, and other modifications. I kept all of these confidential papers on my desk in my locked office on the fifth floor overnight.

By this time Mary Lou, our baby Shannon and I had moved to an apartment in a high-rise in downtown Chicago. Late one night I was awakened by a phone call from the person who was on the air at the time. He said some people were in my office. I questioned how they were able to get into my office because I was sure I left it locked. He said they gained access by coming through the office window!

Outside my office windows was a ledge about 20 to 24 inches wide and between 30 to 40 feet high off the sidewalk. Apparently, some of the jocks and engineers who worked overnight would go out a production studio window facing Michigan Avenue and sit on the ledge for a while. On this night they walked along the ledge to the windows outside my office facing Wacker Drive and opened one of them. They climbed in my window and got back into the station by opening my locked door from the inside. When Paul Abrams heard about this, he went ballistic. He wanted to fire everyone and eventually we had to cut ties with a few people. He was worried that our new format information had been compromised but there was no indication it had been disturbed. It was time for some changes!

I changed the WLS identity from "Rock of Chicago" to "Musicradio WLS" in 1973. I was in New York City meeting with WABC Program Director Rick Sklar and listening to his station. WABC was already using the Musicradio moniker in New York and I thought it was a brilliant idea. Rock of Chicago didn't fit the music that was out at that time. There was such a strong folk influence in the music and a lot of pop songs. I called our morning jock,

Charlie Van Dyke, from New York and asked him to use the phrase "WLS Musicradio" in every break and drop "The Rock of Chicago" jingles. By the time I returned to Chicago the radio station had comfortably adopted the Musicradio theme and the promotion department had some logo artwork ready to be reviewed. In a short amount of time we decided to use both "Musicradio WLS" and "WLS Musicradio."

Charlie told me Chicago's cold winter made him homesick for the west coast. After a little more than a year at WLS, he decided he wanted to go back to Los Angeles and to radio station KHJ. We arranged for a convenient time for both of us to enable him to get out of his contract with WLS and be free to return to L.A. Once it was known he was leaving, I had to find a replacement for Charlie. At that time Fred Winston was doing the 9 a.m.-12 Noon show. Fred wasted no time in coming to me to say he wanted to do the morning show. I questioned him about the hardship lifestyle of morning radio people. It meant he could no longer have late nights in bars and clubs. And there is always a lot of morning show prep before going on the air. The biggest sacrifice is getting little sleep during the week. But Fred wanted to do it. So, I agreed.

Fred is one of the most creative people I've ever worked with. And his real strength is spontaneity. He can be hysterical. On one of his first mornings, Fred arrived at the radio station with reams of show prep paperwork. He had written out some jokes and ideas, but I didn't feel they worked. I asked him not to prepare anything and just come in and react to whatever was happening. There aren't many talented guys who could do this, but Fred Winston is a very rare talent. He is outrageously funny when he is given the freedom to talk to other people. Fred worked with WLS newsman

70

Lyle Dean on an idea called Choose Your News. Lyle would give him 3 headlines of stories and Fred would choose one and then ad-lib and react around it. This was a very funny bit and became a popular tune-in feature.

I went to Marshall Field's department store one day and bought a duck call. It was an accordion manual type duck call and the Chief Engineer, Don Amell, created a device that the thing would fit into. Fred just had to tap it and he used it as a time-tone whenever he gave the time. I told him even if he forgets to tap it when he gives the time of day, tap it whenever you think of it because the audience will be listening for it. Another feature Fred and I developed was *The Answer Lady*. With Fred's incredible deep voice, he'd answer the phone with "Hello, it's the Answer Lady. What's the answer?" The listener would give him a short phrase and Fred would come up with a humorous question to fit it. This was another popular bit with listeners.

Fred and I became first-time fathers around the same time. One Saturday he and I hung out with his son and my daughter who were both toddlers while our wives went shopping together. Fred is a terrific cook and spent the day cooking dinner for the four of us. We asked our wives to stop at a nearby liquor store to buy a bottle of wine. Fred had been preparing a ham on a rotisserie basting it with Pepsi Cola all day. Our wives selected a bottle of a Chateau Lafite-Rothschild priced around $100. They told us when they were in line to pay for it, the cashier questioned them on why they were buying a bottle of expensive wine. He was an older gentleman who thought it necessary to instruct these two young women, in a condescending manner, how to open the bottle allowing it to breathe and how to pour it in a wine glass. After they paid for the wine Fred's wife looked at him and said that they were actually taking it home to mix it with soda water and create a spritzer. They saw the look of shock on the man's face when they left the store and laughed all the way home.

About a year after Larry Lujack left WLS, Paul Abrams arranged a meeting with Lujack and his attorney, Saul Foos, at a restaurant near the two radio stations and he asked me to attend. I don't know if the restaurant was always poorly lit or if Paul requested for it to be that way for secrecy, but we sat in the dark in a booth. Before we walked to the meeting, I questioned him about why we were doing this since I felt Fred Winston was doing a great job. However, I also wanted to know if Larry would come back to WLS to do afternoon drive. The meeting didn't last long, and it was obvious there was no interest from Lujack in returning. I could never figure out why they took the meeting in the first place.

I had many sleepless nights in those days. Not only did we have a young toddler in the apartment, but it seemed like almost every night around 2 or 3 a.m., I would get a phone call from Paul Abrams either asking me if I just heard what the jock said on the air or he'd want to tell me he had an idea for a promotion. One of those promotions was "The Jukebox Idea." After a couple of weeks of these sleepless nights, I told him to stop calling me in the middle of the night. I didn't mind the baby waking me up, but his calls were disturbing the whole family. He agreed and apologized and said I should take Mary Lou to the Top of the Hancock Restaurant and have a nice dinner and he'd arrange to pay for it. We took him up on that offer and had a wonderful dinner with a very expensive bottle of wine. Paul said from now on he would have a list of his comments and ideas waiting for me in the morning.

The Jukebox Idea

As Program Director I had several interesting meetings with people outside of radio. Mostly I talked with clients of the radio station and discussed promotion ideas to help them increase their business. Of all the meetings that I attended there was one that I'll never forget. It wasn't with a client. It wasn't with someone who came to us with an idea. This particular meeting was with someone we contacted who turned out to be well known to the local authorities.

During one of those late-night calls in 1973, Paul asked me to consider doing a promotion called *The Music is on Us*. I was half asleep when he told me what he was thinking. I honestly can't remember what he said but I do remember saying I would discuss it with him in the morning. Once I got to work, I met with him in his office and he told me more about his idea. What it involved was having arrangements with area bars and clubs to enable them to provide their customers the ability to insert a quarter for two plays on their jukeboxes and a third song choice would be added for free and paid for by WLS. During our discussion, we came up with ideas on how we would promote it on the air. We even had an idea of how to promote it in the bars and clubs.

At that time jukeboxes were loaded with 45 rpm records (long before digital) and each record would be in its alphanumeric slot. The idea was to have special 45 rpm records created with a voice recording that would say, "THE MUSIC IS ON US – WLS" and then it would end with a WLS jingle. I had one of the jocks record the message. Those discs would be placed in specific slots in the jukebox. Each jukebox would have a sticker saying "The Music is on us – WLS – put in a quarter for two songs and we'll pay for a third." We were hoping we would be able to have a timer inside the jukebox that would play that record with the announcement once or twice per hour.

Abrams had several hundred 45 rpm records produced. Now it was time to talk to the people responsible for jukeboxes. We called around asking for advice and someone suggested we contact a certain record company executive (whose name escapes me today) who introduced us to someone who could help us.

Arrangements were made to meet with a man who was connected to the jukebox operation and placement. His name was Charles English and we were invited to meet at his office. Paul and I drove to the West Side of Chicago and met with Mr. English and some of his colleagues on the second floor of a building over a record store. While Abrams and I drove to the meeting, I had some concerns about other activities this man might be involved in and I guessed that Paul did too. We would just have to see how the meeting played out.

The office wasn't impressive at all. A basic desk with nothing on it except a telephone, two or three folding chairs, no photos or plaques on the walls. English was dressed in a sport shirt and jacket. His associates were big men in jackets and open collar shirts.

We sat in English's office and asked if we could explain our idea in very simple terms. We looked for his response. Mr. English first said that he controlled every jukebox from Chicago to Las Vegas and he was the right guy to talk to.

We said, "Here's our idea. We want to put a 45-rpm record in every jukebox with the message 'The Music is on US – WLS Musicradio.' This message would be only 10 to 15 seconds long."

Mr. English looked as if he was interested and trying to understand so we continued.

We asked if it was possible to put a timer in the jukebox that would cause the machine to play our 45 rpm record every 30 to 45 minutes. He continued to appear to be interested. Bar patrons would be invited to put a quarter in the jukebox and select two songs and then they'd have the chance to add a third song paid for by WLS. He suddenly looked confused. I went over it again. I said, "Is it possible to ensure there is a timer and some sort of a counter on every jukebox that would keep track of how many quarters were used in the promotion? If so, we would pay a negotiated amount monthly to cover the cost of a 3rd song played." Mr. English just answered, "Yeah." I then asked how reliable the counter would be and who would provide that information. English said his people would service the jukeboxes and get the necessary information. I asked if he felt confident about the accuracy and he responded loudly, "Nobody fucks with Chuckie English." I guess that shows just how naïve I was!

I also mentioned that by using this idea, English could have a new source of revenue. I expected him to get excited about this, but he just looked at me and asked, "How?" I told him his people could approach tobacco, beer, and liquor companies to sell advertising on his jukeboxes. A timer could be set to have a 15 to a 30-second commercial announcement on a 45-rpm record and it would play in the bars and clubs for point-of-purchase advertising. The Federal Communications Commission had banned all cigarette advertising over radio and television in 1971 but most tobacco companies had catchy jingles they used previously on radio and television: "Winston tastes good like a (clap clap) cigarette should,"

"L.S.M.F.T. – Lucky Strike means fine tobacco", "You're in Marlboro Country" and more.

After we explained the whole idea, English said, "Let's go to lunch." So, we followed him to a small Italian restaurant nearby and when we got there, the owner led us to a private room. The owner's daughter was our waitress and a lavish lunch was served. English asked me to explain the timer idea again and I did, and he just couldn't understand how it would work. I remember he kept calling us "WCFL" instead of WLS. We kept correcting him, but it didn't make a difference.

I should mention one more thing of interest in this meeting. This lunch occurred during the Watergate hearings in Washington, DC. We discussed what we were hearing in the news and English said it was his opinion that the one security guard who supposedly caught the ex-CIA agents in the Democratic Party Headquarters in the Watergate complex couldn't have possibly held them there without it being a set-up.

English told us a story that he, Al Capone and one other person were at a brothel when it was raided by the Chicago Police. One armed officer was holding the three of them in a room waiting for a paddy wagon to take them in for booking when Capone told the officer, "This will be very embarrassing to our families, so I suggest you look the other way and we'll be leaving. And if you don't, then there's no way you can shoot the three of us." English said the officer turned and left the room and the three men left without any problem.

We left lunch that day thinking the jukebox idea had some life, but I wasn't convinced he really understood it. English did say he'd think about it. Now it was time for Paul to inform his boss,

Charles DeBare – President of ABC Owned Radio Stations. Chuck DeBare was previously General Counsel for Owned and Operated ABC Radio Stations. It was a time when many radio stations' FCC Licenses were being challenged all around the country by women's groups and other organizations claiming the stations were not truly acting in the public interest. When DeBare heard the jukebox idea, Abrams told me he was instructed to drop it. We wound up passing out the 45 rpm records to people on the street outside the Stone Container Building, which at that time was at the corner of Michigan Avenue and Wacker Drive.

We learned later that we were both very naïve. The man we met with Charles "Chuckie" English was one of the top enforcers for The Outfit. He was a North Side guy who specialized in jukeboxes and vending machines. During Sam Giancana's reign as top Chicago Boss, he was considered a lieutenant. He eventually was gunned down in February 1985.

Raiding a Shop

In 1973 I made several changes to the air talent. Jim Kerr was doing the morning show on the ABC FM station in Chicago, WDAI. I asked Jim if he would like to join WLS. I told him I was going to hire several people who were currently on FM stations and I needed him to do weekends, fill-in work and production. Jim agreed and was an important member of the staff. He left WLS in 1974 to do mornings at a major New York City radio station. His first day in NYC was the day after he rode the WLS Float in the St. Patrick's Day Parade. Jim is still on the air in New York. In 2018, I was very happy to learn that he was inducted into the National Radio Hall of Fame.

I was able to hire three FM air talents and one great music director. 1973 was a time that radio markets were beginning to feel the growth of the audience on FM radio stations at the expense of AM stations. In discussions with the WLS General Manager and colleagues at ABC Radio in New York, I thought the jocks that were gaining in the ratings on FM could be the ones to fill the positions on WLS and therefore slow the pace of FM growth in Chicago.

First priority: Get the air-talent situation fixed. After hiring Jim Kerr, the 2 a.m.-5:30 a.m. show was open, and I approached Yvonne Daniels at WSDM-FM about coming to WLS to take over that show. She would be moving from evenings at WSDM to overnights at WLS. When Paul Abrams and I met with Yvonne and her attorney I explained that WLS considered the overnight show very special because our 50,000-watt clear channel signal could be heard almost coast to coast, up in Canada and parts of Mexico. I told them we also regularly receive fan mail from Europe. After a series of proposals, Yvonne agreed to the terms of a contract and joined the WLS lineup.

Shortly after I hired Yvonne, the 10 p.m. – 2 a.m. shift opened, and we contacted Bob Sirott at WBBM-FM. Bob's brother Herb was his agent and we offered that late night show to Bob and he accepted. He made an immediate impact and sounded great! He was only in that time slot for a brief time. We lost our music director/midday talent due to a company policy violation and I decided to move JJ Jeffrey from afternoon drive to middays. So now we needed to put someone in the very important afternoon shift who would compete with our Top 40 rival WCFL and "Super-jock" Larry Lujack. Bob seemed to be the ideal choice because he was young, a lifelong Chicagoan, very creative and he sounded totally different than Lujack. Bob took ownership of that shift and was on top of the current events everyone was talking about.

With Bob moving to afternoons, that left the 10 p.m.-2 a.m. shift open. I went back to WBBM-FM and hired Steve King. Steve fit perfectly in that late-night slot being heard all over the Midwest and beyond. His knowledge of the music provided the ideal content between the songs.

Now that the air-talent was in place, the new question was: What am I going to do for a Music Director? That was easy – contact Jim Smith at WBBM-FM and lure him over to the Big 89. I'm proud of all the hiring decisions I made – especially this one because in retrospect Smith brought his wisdom and experience to one of the most critical positions at any music radio station. He was respected by the record industry. He was honest and meticulous when creating the music charts and music rotations.

One more thing about Steve King. He was a very valuable air talent not only as a jock, but he became one of the main hosts of *MusicPeople*, which was an interview program of rock stars that I created. Recording artists would often stop by the studios to promote a new album or appearance and we'd arrange beforehand to have them sit with one of our jocks for an interview. Once we had the raw audio of the interview, Jim Smith would work with production engineer, Alan Rosen, and produce a one-hour show of the interview and the artist's music. The program ran on Sunday nights at 10 o'clock and was very successful.

The term "raiding a shop" is what happened at WBBM-FM. There were two reasons that I did this. First, the talent I was able to lure away to WLS was exceptional and second, WBBM-FM and WSDM-FM were beginning to make inroads in the ratings. In fact, all FM radio was making inroads in the ratings and bringing those talented people to WLS delayed the eventual penetration of FM radio listening in Chicago. The Windy City was the last of the major cities in the U.S. to have FM superiority in radio ratings.

Jeff Davis eventually replaced Steve King after a few years. Jeff came to WLS from the East Coast and became the voice of the radio station's public service announcements. They all ended with his tag line, "WLS, getting it said for Chicago." His voice could be heard from coast to coast and throughout the rest of North America. Jeff is one of those rare talents who sounds great in any air-shift and production piece.

So, the air-talent and the music department were all set. Now the radio station had to deal with a movement that was beginning to affect the entire industry.

Local and senior management were worried about individuals and organizations challenging our FCC License. It was not uncommon for various groups to be upset about radio station's programming content. Were radio stations addressing the needs of the local community? Was radio management programming content specifically targeted to the population of their city of license? These were all of the areas each American radio station promised to focus on to prove they are operating in the public interest.

The Women's Movement was gaining momentum and the National Organization of Women (NOW) had already challenged some radio station licenses in a few big cities. At that time Paul Abrams was the General Manager of WLS. He reached out to the local chapter of NOW and offered to have them write or otherwise provide input to a special show called *The Women of Rock n Roll* that we would assist in creating and producing. The executives of the local chapter appreciated and accepted the offer. I worked with representatives of NOW and collectively we wrote the script, selected the music and produced a three-hour special that WLS ran on a Sunday morning. It was hosted by WLS personality Yvonne Daniels.

They also requested that WLS hire and train a woman with no radio experience to host a show. We agreed to that. I asked a local talent agency to send a few women who had done voice-over work but no on-air radio experience to audition for this training position. I can't recall how many women auditioned for the job, but I hired Daphne Maxwell to be the trainee. She did a great job of watching, listening, and rehearsing on tape over a few months and eventually, she hosted a late-night show on weekends.

More Changes

All of us at WLS had fun in the summer of 1973 out with the public. The radio station had a Volkswagen "Thing" automobile. We hired a driver and named him "Citizen Ken." We also hired a hot girl to ride with him and we named her "Connie Thunderbody." Remember, this was back in the 70's! They made appearances all over Chicagoland that drew huge crowds. We had a pilot who flew over the city towing a huge WLS sign and we referred to him as "Captain Rockover." We had personalities everywhere. The jocks had fun talking about these characters on the air throughout the summer.

Paul Abrams was removed from the General Manager position in September, 1973 and Martin Greenberg arrived from Detroit to succeed him. Marty was a breath of fresh air. He was highly respected in the ABC organization and he was very personable to the staff of WLS. We went through other changes at the radio station with a new

General Sales Manager, National Sales Manager and new additions to the sales staff. Many of our sales members were Greek which led to most of our sales parties being held in Greektown. OPA!

The radio station made lots of money. One example of that was a young sales guy who told me that when he arrived at WLS, he just sat at his desk and wrote orders. His name was Simon T. He would work a six-day week and that meant on Saturdays he would come in and take orders over the phone. We even had a Saturday receptionist. Simon went on to be a very successful broadcast executive that I would end up competing with later in our careers. Luckily the competition never affected our friendship.

Shortly after Marty Greenberg arrived, he asked me how we could grow. I suggested that we try to lure Larry Lujack back to WLS. He liked the idea but first, he needed to get approval from ABC Legal. We knew Larry was under contract at WCFL and we didn't want to tamper with the contract. We also didn't want Larry to get in trouble. Once he got approval from ABC lawyers, Marty called Saul Foos and requested a meeting. They didn't hesitate to agree to a meeting in Foos's office. I introduced Marty to the two of them and we talked about the possibility of Larry returning to WLS. They declined the offer, but they left us with the impression it wasn't totally out of the question. Their attitude was far different from the meeting I had with them and Paul Abrams. I think both Foos and Larry were impressed with Greenberg. They knew immediately that he was different than Abrams. In the end, Foos and Larry said they were not interested in pursuing an agreement. As we got up to leave, Marty turned and said, "It would be nice to have you back at WLS Larry, but in any event, we'll just have to win without you." That's exactly what we did.

Another programming element I created was the Touch Tone Contest. That was the new technology with phones at the time, since they were no longer rotary phones but touch-tone phones. I was playing around in my office one day and I replicated the musical signature of WLS on the phone. The numbers were 8-5-2-0-5. Al Rosen carted it up and from that point on it became the cue for listeners to call in and win a prize.

A feature we ran every New Year's Eve at the stroke of midnight was The Montage. It was an ever-growing series of song snippets from the 50s to the present day. Those quickly edited song segments started in a program I wrote in early 1973 called The Souvenir Years. The first broadcast of The Montage was New Year's Eve 1973. Jim Kerr was the jock who introduced it for the first time. The feature included short segments of all the hit songs for the years between 1955 and 1973. Every year of music was about 60 seconds long. Al Rosen was responsible for the incredible edits and crossfades. We added music every year until I left WLS.

In late 1973 we launched a major on-air contest called Gotcha. For the introduction we hired an actor to do an imitation of Groucho Marx's voice and called the character: Gotcha. This contest centered on "Gotcha here at WLS. If we call and ask the name of your favorite radio station, say WLS and you will win!" It was a phenomenal success. After a while, I changed the name to the Musicradio Game and retired Gotcha. Over time we gave away everything from t-shirts to albums, concert tickets, sailboats, cars and we even sent dozens of families to Walt Disney World in Orlando. The Musicradio Game had a multi-year life on WLS.

I was very proud of what we accomplished but the stress was getting to me. I had taken a pay cut from the position as production director and on-air personality, both under a union contract, to be the program director. I talked it over with General Manager Marty Greenberg who was very understanding. I decided to resign. I planned on leaving WLS but agreed to stay until a replacement was named. Marty accepted the resignation and soon called me in to say that he had hired John Gehron from WCBS-FM in New York to replace me. John invited me to dinner where he asked if I'd stay at WLS and assist him as the Production Director, so I agreed. John let me have the freedom to come up with contests and ideas with our promotion department. Furthermore, John allowed guys like Fred Winston, John Landecker, Bob Sirott, Steve King and others to be very creative on their shows. It was a golden time at WLS. Creativity was everywhere, and we all helped each other to try new ideas.

The WLS air-staff was very much in tune with what was going on in the streets. New fads were popping up and one of the craziest was "streaking." Students were shedding all their clothes and running across university campuses. Weekend jock Jim Kerr was asked to cover the phenomena on the Northwestern campus in Evanston. He did a great job of recording interviews and making phone call reports. We thought we had that fad covered but Bob Sirott came up with the best idea yet. He decided (with our concurrence) that he wanted to raise money for The Muscular Dystrophy Association. If he achieved the goal of $500, he would streak across the Michigan Avenue Bridge at 5 p.m. on a Friday. The contributions started coming in and Bob said the streak was going to happen.

We contacted the Chicago Police Department and told them what the plan was, and their commander told us there's no way he could allow Bob to run naked across the bridge. Mayor Daley wouldn't like it. No way! We developed a plan to have Bob in a pair of flesh-colored shorts with a large blanket around him. Before he threw off the blanket, the commander would ask him how much money it would take to meet Bob's goal. Then the commander would pull out cash and say he was donating the final amount as long as Bob agreed not to streak. Bob would take the money, thank the commander and say he was going to streak anyway and start to take off the blanket. Two officers would stop that from happening and hustle Bob to a nearby squad car and leave.

The plan was set. John Landecker took over Bob's show that afternoon. John had a great line I'll never forget. He asked the question on the air, "Are we in for a big surprise or a little surprise?"

Bob took the elevator down to the lobby and was met by a WLS salesman whose client was The Wrigley Gum Company. He asked Bob if he would carry a giant inflatable pack of Wrigley Spearmint Gum when he streaked the bridge. Bob declined because he was more worried about what he'd gotten himself into. As Bob left the WLS building, he saw the huge crowd outside waiting on the Michigan Avenue Bridge. It included Channel 7 WLS-TV cameras and reporter Tim Weigel ready to cover the stunt. The plan went off perfectly.

Once Bob was in the squad car, he was driven around for a while until the crowd thinned out. Landecker fielded phone calls from Bob's fans worried that he had been arrested, but he had been secretly ushered back into the WLS building. We kept Bob off the air for a while and eventually he went back on the air and said he was OK and wasn't in any trouble. It was a great promotion thanks to Bob's creativity and the Chicago Police Department.

Since this event took place between the *Chicago Tribune* and The *Chicago Sun-Times* buildings, we had massive publicity. It was the lead item in Aaron Gold's Tower Ticker column in the March 14th, 1974 edition of the Trib. And of course, we had the television coverage from Channel 7 that everyone was talking about.

It was the beginning of the end of WCFL'S competitive edge with Larry Lujack in the afternoons. I believe this promotion was the turning point in the ratings. Much later I asked Larry about that stunt and in a typical Lujack response he said, "He didn't beat me, WLS beat WCFL."

Before the Bob Sirott streak of the bridge, everyone in media and advertising paid much more attention to the competition of radio morning shows. But since Bob was up against Larry Lujack, the publicity generated by this stunt threw a spotlight on Bob and WLS became a major competitor again in the afternoon.

Bob Sirott occasionally called us in the morning to request some production studio time before his afternoon show. He wanted some sound effects for his features that day. Bob had bits like *The BS Love Counselor*, *The BS Horoscope* and using "OPA!" with the 5 o'clock horn of happiness.

John Landecker, in particular, had an overabundance of creativity in his evening show. He followed the music format of the radio station but what he did between the songs was new, innovative and revolutionary. One of the terms that people were using at that time was "let's boogie." John created *Boogie Check* to check your boogie. To keep the feature to a reasonable amount of time, we created a cart with a few minutes of dead air then Fred Winston's excited high-pitched voice would announce: "Stop it... AHH Stop it... Terminate this AHH Boogie Check OOOH" at which time John would stop taking calls and award a prize. There were several unique terms that John created in answering live calls and responding to listener's questions and comments. John would answer the phone with "Are you talkin' to me? About what?" That found its way into our house. One night at dinner I asked my young daughter a question. She responded: "Are you talkin' to me? About what?" We burst out laughing. John's creative talents were showcased in his spontaneity in dealing with his audience. The phone lines were always overloaded with people wanting to get on *Boogie Check*. The feature became more and more popular and, in most cases, the engineer wouldn't start the dead air cart until John flashed a hand-cue, so it continued longer.

John's creativity didn't stop there. He created musical features using character voices asking news conference type questions with the answers being snippets of popular songs.

The mood in every department at WLS was electric. Our radio station sounded brilliant. I can't help but feel Marty's presence brought new energy to the station. But more changes were about to come.

What's Your Favorite Radio Station?

In 1975 a representative from Walt Disney World in Florida asked to meet with the creative staff of WLS to discuss his idea of a promotion. He told us his research showed that people on the West Coast would likely vacation at Disneyland in California. Everyone on the East Coast would likely vacation at Walt Disney World in Florida. He wanted everyone in the Midwest to also consider vacationing at Walt Disney World. The plan was to give away dozens and dozens of family trips on Amtrak to Disney World in Orlando, all expenses paid.

We loved the idea. We told him we would come up with something and contact him. There were a couple of contest ideas, but it was obvious that we already had THE contest – "The Musicradio Game – What's Your Favorite Radio Station?" We pitched the idea to him, and he loved it.

I did all the promos for the contest and they all had to be approved by Disney World executives. I wrote scripts for the character voices of Goofy and Mickey Mouse. They were recorded in Florida after approval from Disney. I used the Jiminy Cricket song of "When You Wish Upon A Star" as the musical theme of the contest and the response was enormous. I was told that it was the first radio promotion done outside of Orlando for Disney World. The contest was done later by other radio stations around the Midwest on a much smaller scale and I provided the production elements.

The Disney executive brought two actors who played the costumed characters of Mickey Mouse and Donald Duck to Chicago to help promote the contest. They spent a day in costume visiting children in several hospitals. Later that evening, our Promotion Director, G. Michael Donovan, who had been with the group all day called me at home. He asked if they could all come over to our place. Of course, I said yes, and everyone came to our apartment in a downtown high-rise building. After such a busy day they needed some time to chill and relax. The plan was they would go back to the hotel to change and freshen up which gave Mary Lou and me time to put out some food and drinks for everyone. We had a fun evening. They loved the view we had of the Chicago skyline especially during the brief electrical storm that happened while they were there.

WLS made a connection with area high schools in the late '70s. We arranged for the 7-UP distributor to sponsor the "WLS – 7UP High School Team of the Week." One of the sports reporters for the *Chicago Sun-Times* would select a high school basketball or football team as the Team of the Week. One of the jocks from WLS would go to the school and present the trophy at a game or an assembly. I went to several of these events but the one I remember most was a basketball game at Westinghouse High School on the West Side of Chicago. I had the chance to present the award at half-time but more importantly, it gave me the opportunity to watch their star player in action. It was senior, Mark Aguirre. He was later named College Player of the Year when he played for DePaul University. He would go on to be a two-time NBA Champion and a three-time NBA All-Star.

We Finally Got Him Back

In 1976 a major shift occurred in Chicago radio. Legendary rock n roll station WCFL changed to a format called "Beautiful Music." This was a station with significant heritage with some great names in broadcasting: John Rook, Bob Dearborn, "World Famous" Tom Murphy, Doug Dahlgren, Dick Orkin, "Big" Ron O'Brien, Kris Erik Stevens, Dick Biondi, Clark Weber, Ron Britain, Jim Stagg, Joel Sebastian, Barney Pipp, and of course Larry "Superjock" Lujack were just a few of the many iconic names in Chicago radio that called CFL their home. The era of AM radio dominance in Chicago was beginning to come to an end. I've always attributed that to the great battles between the two

50,000-watt stations: WLS and WCFL and when I hired the best FM talents to come to WLS.

Larry was one of the few jocks to stay at WCFL after the format switch because of his huge no-cut contract. They could only fire him for cause. He told me later that the management at CFL was looking for any excuse to fire him and save money. He made sure he was never late; he always kept an accurate program log and followed the format precisely. It was obvious that WCFL wanted to unload Larry's big contract so that was the opening for WLS to step in and finally get Larry back to the Big 89.

Lew Witz was the General Manager of WCFL. He initiated a call to Marty Greenberg asking if WLS would like to take over Larry's contract. He said he'd be willing to continue to pay Larry a portion of his salary. Marty told Witz that he would have to check with ABC Legal, but he liked the idea. Marty was able to get approval from ABC lawyers who helped draw up the appropriate agreement.

It turned out to be the right time to get Larry back to WLS because there were more changes to come. Fred Winston left WLS and went to work at WFYR and that meant we needed a new morning guy. In 1975 JJ Jeffrey had left the radio station for an ownership position on the East Coast and that opened up the midday show. John Gehron offered me that air-shift, so I left the production director job and Bill Price was hired to replace me. In 1976 Mary Lou was now pregnant with our second child and we decided it was time to buy a house. We moved to a small home in Arlington Heights and our daughter Amy was born a couple of months later. I was doing the midday shift when Larry returned to WLS to do mornings. It was then that I began to hang out in the studio before my show and have fun with Lujack in his final half-hour. That led to...

Animal Stories™

The most popular feature on WLS during the late 70s and early 80s was *Animal Stories*. This evolved from daily farm news in the early days of WLS. Before the mid 1970's WLS had an obligation in the FCC License to do one minute of agriculture news early in the morning. The 50,000-watt clear-channel signal could be heard throughout the Midwest at that time of day. Before Larry Lujack left for WCFL, he was doing the morning show and would read 60 seconds of Ag News in the 5 a.m. hour that would consist of hog prices, wheat prices and different federal and state stories about farm life.

When Larry returned to WLS he no longer had to read Ag News in the morning. Every morning I would go into the main air studio where Larry was in the last half hour of his 5:30 a.m. – 10 a.m. shift and pull my oldies. That meant I would take a large loose-leaf binder that contained the title, artist, cart number and year of release of every oldie we had in our library. Each jock would initial and date the song title to show when it was played. Those would be the oldies we would play that day. We would pull the respective carts from the wall rack and give them to the board operators. While I was selecting the oldies, I would sit on Larry's left in a newsperson's chair. We'd talk off-mic during the songs about whatever was on our mind. Larry had several live commercials for True Value Hardware Stores and other clients each morning around 9:30 a.m.

By the way, management told us that we shouldn't play with the True Value Hardware script because the client wouldn't like it. Larry mentioned that on the air once and the True Value executive reportedly called to say he wanted us to have fun with the commercial since those 60 second spots were lasting 90 seconds or more! Sometimes I would open my microphone and ask a question or say something stupid while he was reading the commercial and we would both start laughing. I think that was the beginning of what would become *Animal Stories*.

One morning when I went into the studio at the normal time, Larry said he had a couple of stories about some farm animals and I should sit down, and we'd do a bit about them. He said he'd introduce it this way: "Gather the moppets around the radio, Moms and Dads, for Uncle Lar's *Animal Stories* with his little friend, Little Tommy." I said, "Yeah, OK. And call me something like little snot-nose Tommy." That was the first *Animal Stories* broadcast and our program director John Gehron said he thought it was funny. Over time the feature got longer and longer because we were having so much fun. John Gehron said he thought it was going too long and to trim it down. Larry mentioned that on the next broadcast, and we cut the bit short. The switchboard lit up with complaints. Everyone said this feature was too funny to cut short. Eventually John told us, "Just go with it."

In the beginning the *Animal Stories* broadcasts featured stories I was hearing for the first time live. Larry suggested we experiment with me looking at the stories before the broadcast. That turned out to be a big mistake. They just weren't that funny when I knew what was coming. Also, Larry had a unique style of storytelling. He'd use long pauses and a slow cadence that would emphasize funny passages of the story that would make them even funnier. We stopped the experiment and he kept the stories and pictures hidden so I wouldn't see them until we were live on the air.

He would occasionally set me up to sound really stupid. One morning before we went live, he said he had a story about a dog on the railroad tracks. He said, "And make sure you say, dog gonna be OK?" I agreed. Once we were on the air, he read a story about a dog walking along the railroad tracks about the same time a commuter train was arriving. He looked over at me and I said, "Dog gonna be ok, Uncle Lar?" He paused for a moment and said, "No, you moron! Dog not gonna be OK. I just told you the train was arriving." I realized he had set me up and I stifled a laugh. He loved doing that.

Animal Stories was instantly popular. The first *Animal Stories* T-Shirt the promotion department created was a rooster wearing a hat with the word "press" on it. The bird was inside a circle that said "Uncle Lar's *Animal Stories* on WLS." That created a problem for me. I was upset there was no mention of me in the promotion and I voiced my complaint to both John Gehron and the promotion director. I was told it wasn't going to change so I told Larry I was not going to be in future episodes of *Animal Stories*. I admit that I was being vain, but I felt it was important to stand up for myself.

Larry used the fact I wasn't on the feature anymore on the air in the introductions saying something like, "That spotlight over there is empty since Li'l Tommy is upset he's not included on T-shirts, so he has resigned from *Animal Stories*."

It took only a couple of days until the new *Animal Stories* T-shirt came out showing two cute little beavers. One identified as Uncle Lar' and the other as Li'l Tommy. I came back to the show and everyone was happy.

We started to receive huge amounts of mail at that point. People would write stories about their strange experiences with animals and they'd cut out articles from hometown newspapers. Some of the letters were written very creatively. And of course, Larry would spend hours and hours going over all the mail and select only a few stories for each day. When one of us would go on vacation, we'd work ahead and record a number of broadcasts on reel-to-reel tape.

Other than those days, each broadcast was performed live and a board-operator would roll tape on it. Once Larry got off the air, he and the board-op would edit the tape for a rerun the next morning. The live broadcast was at 9:45 a.m. and would run anywhere from 4 minutes to 10 minutes. The rerun would be at 6:45 a.m. the next business day since many people started their workday earlier.

It wasn't long until businesses and factories would call the station to complain that their workers would be out in the parking lot listening to their car radios and wouldn't come to work until *Animal Stories* was over. Those managers were asking our bosses to shorten our broadcasts so their workers would arrive on time. We were fortunate that our managers realized that *Animal Stories* would work best when they allowed us to be creative.

WLS had a wonderful relationship with the Plitt Movie Theater chain in the Chicago area thanks to a fellow by the name of Jerry Bulger. Jerry, a Plitt executive, was a big fan of Larry and used him as the star of a short film that was shown before the main feature. Larry wore a WLS sweater and was holding a box of popcorn. As he was about to open the door to the big screen theater, he looked at the camera and said that he'd be sitting in the back row and if you were good boys and girls and didn't talk during the movie and didn't throw trash on the floor, after the movie he might reward you with a shiny new dime if you could find him.

Speaking of shiny new dimes, how many of those did I miss out on? *Animal Stories Quiz* was a regular feature of the program where Uncle Lar' would offer Li'l Tommy a chance to win a shiny new dime if he could answer a quiz question. I can only remember winning once. It had to do with a story about toilet seats in outhouses. The question was, "Why are the woodchucks eating outhouse toilet seats?" I guessed it was because of the salt from sweaty bottoms. I was right so Larry pulled a dime out of his pocket and paid me. The rest of the time I either guessed wrong or he made sure I'd lose. One example I'll never forget was, "What color is a polar bear's fur?" I remember saying, "I got this! That's easy. It's white." And I remember Lar' saying, "That's a good guess Li'l Tommy but it's wrong. A polar bear's fur is translucent." "What? That's not a color!" By that time, he was ending the show with "That's all the time we have for Animal Stories today, boys and girls….." I never told Lar' that fans were sending me shiny new dimes in the mail almost every day.

Meanwhile *Animal Stories* became so popular, Larry and I were asked to do another film for the Plitt Theaters. Larry told me he could hypnotize a chicken. We came up with the idea of him telling the audience that if they promised not to talk during the movie or smoke or throw trash, he would do a trick of hypnotizing a chicken. A few years later he told me he had never done that before and he had only heard people talk about being able to do it. The day we shot the film he said he was nervous it wouldn't work. Well, it did work. Larry gently pushed the chicken's head down to the console of the radio control board and slowly drew a straight line away from the chicken's beak. Once he released the chicken's head, the bird was frozen. It wouldn't move. It was hypnotized! Then I would say, "Wow! Nice trick Uncle Lar." Then he'd close it by saying, "Ok, remember you promised. I thank you, Li'l Tommy thanks you..." and I'd say, "And the chicken thanks you." But the problem was the darn chicken was still frozen with its head down on the console and its back end sticking up. We didn't want to leave it that way, so we needed to wake the chicken up. I said I'd goose it when I picked it up. We rolled film for a final take because we could only do that once. And, sure enough when I said, "The chicken thanks you" I squeezed a little on its belly and the chicken sprung to life and began flapping its wings and tried to fly away. But of course, chickens can't fly so it jumped from my hands and wound up on a coat tree. That film was the most popular trailer we ever did.

Shortly after that film was introduced in all the Plitt Theaters, Shannon our oldest daughter who had just started junior high, came home from an afternoon at the movies with friends almost in tears. We asked her what was wrong, and she said that she was so embarrassed because she and her friends watched the film of me with Larry hypnotizing a chicken. Her friends liked it, especially seeing me wearing a baseball hat with antlers. They laughed and even pointed to me on the screen. We asked her why she was embarrassed, and she said that everyone in the theatre was laughing at us. We assured her that it was OK because the audience was supposed to laugh, and we were happy to hear that they did, and Larry would be too. That made her feel a lot better, but it was only one of the many times I embarrassed my children!

Over the next few years we did a few more films for Plitt Theaters. The next one was a takeoff of *At the Movies* with Gene

Siskel and Roger Ebert. This time Larry and I were in theater seats and we were showing examples of humorous bad behavior in the theater. The next two films featured all of the WLS DJs in "Bigfoot." A rough looking guy was smoking and talking during the movie and all of us show up wearing big foot type shoes to escort him out of the theater.

During the summer of 1979, there was a huge anti-disco movement in Chicago. WLS was playing all the popular music of the day and many songs had a disco themed sound. Disco Demolition occurred at Comiskey Park that year and soon after, our promotional vans were being belted with rocks and eggs when our jocks went out on personal appearances. Each of the two vans was called "The Magic Bus" after the song by The Who. But since WLS was playing disco songs along with popular rock songs, our vans were the target of the anti-disco movement. We needed to change things. At a jock meeting we recommended the station repaint the vans and label them *Animal Stories* Mobile Units. Overnight everything changed. The public gave us thumbs up and the vans became extremely popular. Pools, festivals and clients were calling the station begging for us to make appearances at their events. Baskin-Robbins Ice Cream even named an ice-cream flavor after *Animal Stories* one summer and we gave out samples all summer long.

Animal Stories rarely had guests on the show but in one instance Illinois Governor James Thompson surprised us by walking into the studio during a broadcast. He mentioned he was a big fan and we invited him to put on some headphones and stay. We teased him and he gave it right back to us. The Governor sent us invitations to his official Christmas party in Springfield later that year. We were honored by the invitation, but Larry and I decided that we didn't want to drive more than 3 hours each way to Springfield just for a 2-hour cocktail party. We both had to go on the air the next day. Needless to say, our wives were very disappointed!

We continued to receive photographs and stories from our fans including hometown newspaper clippings. Larry would identify the sender as an *Animal Stories* News Team Correspondent. Some letters were written very creatively, and some would request that they be named *Animal Stories* Bureau Chief of their community. Larry would usually say that title is reserved for people who show us their qualifications. As you can imagine, photos of topless women began pouring into the station and each broadcast would feature Larry showing me the latest application for bureau chief. That would get me giggling and that usually set the mood for that day's broadcast. One morning Larry mentioned we had a new application for Bureau Chief, and he handed me a photo of a bare breasted older woman with boobs down to her waist. That got me laughing and then he said she was Miss Cal-Sag Channel of 1977 and that caused me to lose it. I was laughing so hard and pounding on the desk and that caused Larry to sound as if he was stifling a laugh and then losing it himself and kicking the metal trash can. Now the listeners were picturing what that photo looked like and I'm sure they were laughing too.

After a while we had enough tape of funny stories that Larry and I wanted to put out an album. We approached management and they agreed on the condition that we give 100% of the profits to charity. They also wanted to approve all content before the album went into production. Larry and I were fans of Jack Mabley of the *Chicago Tribune*. He was a writer who had a favorite charity called The Forgotten Children's Fund. This charity raised money for children and adults of various ages in mental health facilities. More importantly every single dollar went to buy things like toothpaste, soap and other items including stuffed animals and toys for the patients.

The work behind creating these vinyl albums involved Larry and me having to listen to hours of *Animal Stories* with the help of WLS board-op Rene Tondelli. We selected the stories we wanted, and Rene would piece them together in the order the three of us decided on. This was long before digital editing, so Rene had to use a razor blade to splice the audio tape around each story. The transitions from some stories into others were a challenge because of how much laughter was involved. Larry or I would rustle some paper or make other background noises to bridge the tracks to make it sound as if all of the stories occurred in one broadcast.

By the way, Rene went on to become an expert in sound editing in Hollywood and was nominated for an Academy Award for Best Sound Editing for the 2016 film *Deepwater Horizon*. She has worked on a number of major motion pictures in her career including *Mary Poppins Returns* in 2018 and *Bombshell* in 2019.

Over the next several years we put out three vinyl albums at WLS and all of the money went to the Forgotten Children's Fund. I was told we made over $250,000 for the fund in the sale of three volumes of Animal Stories.

In 1984 Larry and I received an award for contributing and helping children with special needs from Eunice Kennedy Shriver.

Releasing the three vinyl albums gave us the opportunity to join the National Academy of Recording Arts and Sciences (NARAS) now known as The Recording Academy. This organization began in 1957 and is known for the Grammy Awards along with various music foundations. We were now privileged to vote for the awards and be eligible for nomination. Somehow, that Grammy Nomination never happened, but that didn't stop us from suggesting it might. Larry dropped out of NARAS a year later and I was asked to join the Board of Governors of the local chapter. During my time on the Board I arranged a seminar for local musicians to hear Program Directors from many of the major Chicago radio stations describe their policies on selecting what records to play on the air. Some of these musicians and producers had told me they couldn't understand why local radio wasn't obligated to play local artists. The Program Directors explained how and why they selected the songs to play in their respective formats. It was a very educational experience.

In the late 1970s or early 1980s, Larry told me he was approached by a Chicago television station about doing something on Saturday nights. He told me he shot down the idea because it was "too much work and it would interfere with golf." All of his fans knew how important golf was. He even played with snow on the ground in bitter cold temperatures! He would be the only person on the course.

By the mid-90's, *Animal Stories* had been off the air for just over a decade and all the while Larry and I had all the master tapes. They had been stored in their original 8-inch tape boxes and placed in a large plastic tub to protect them from the elements. By this time, I was living in California and was working for CBS as Program Director of KCBS-FM in Los Angeles.

Rick Dees, a very popular morning jock at radio station KIIS-FM in LA, called and invited me to lunch. He asked if he could borrow the *Animal Stories* tapes to listen to. He wanted to get ideas for a new on-air feature he was creating called "Ranger Rick." We agreed on a fee for this privilege and Rick took temporary custody of them.

One day I called Larry and asked him if he'd be interested in going in with me in releasing some of the stories on CD. His immediate reaction was that it was too much work and he wasn't interested in investing any of his own funds in the production and marketing of the CDs. He told me to go ahead with the project if I wanted to. He said he doubted we'd ever make that much money because he didn't think many people would want to buy them.

I arranged with a firm in Canada to produce the CDs. They eventually shipped Volume 1 which was the same audio that was on our first vinyl album. I contacted the Program Director of WLS and told him my plans and he arranged to have me interviewed on their popular morning show and sales took off.

Attorney Scott Zolke encouraged us to protect the *Animal Stories* name. He did the paperwork to file the name with the federal government. So, we own the service mark.

Mary Lou took over the whole project of sales, shipping and accounting and it became her full-time job. She took care of everything!

Eventually we released an additional four volumes of CDs. Several years after I began selling them, Larry called and said he wanted to talk about sharing the profits henceforth. Earlier he had said he had no problem with me keeping it all since I had made all of the financial investments and did all the work. We agreed on a per-unit figure and Mary Lou would send Larry a check every month. He would often joke that it was the highlight of his month when he'd open the mailbox and find an envelope with Mary Lou's return address.

Each of the three vinyl albums had its own original artwork. The three framed artwork paintings hung in the WLS Lobby for years. Later they were kept in the basement of the Stone Container Building at Michigan Avenue and Wacker Drive. There came a time when WLS wanted to clean out their storeroom in preparation of moving to a WLS TV building on State Street. I contacted the WLS General Manager at the time and asked if I could have the framed artwork and he agreed. But someone got to them first. It's too bad. I would have loved to have them.

I do have the original artwork for the CDs hanging in my home. Fortunately, I have an artist in the family. My daughter Shannon married Patrick Bobillo who created the artwork for all of the CDs.

Even after *Animal Stories* was off the air, it still had an influence on some friends in the news business. Ron Magers of WLS-TV would often say when covering a story about an animal, "He's gonna be fine, Li'l Tommy." And Dan Gire of the *Daily Herald* wrote a movie review in the October 11, 1996 edition for *The Ghost and the Darkness* as if it was an Animal Story. The subtitle was "This 'Jaws' with claws is full of flaws, Li'l Tommy." Here is a sample: **Lar: Kilmer tries to build this bridge over the Tsavo River in Kenya so the Brits can finish a 580-mile railroad from the Indian Ocean to Lake Victoria. That way, they have access to the lucrative ivory trade.**

Tommy: Wow! All that work just to get bars of soap!

Lar: You amuse me, Li'l Tommy. Anyway, the whole project comes to a grinding halt when these two lions start mistaking the workers for Big Macs. My favorite part comes when a lion grabs the first guy right out of his tent and drags him off into the distance screaming and yelling.

Tommy: Worker gonna be alright, Uncle Lar?

Lar: No, Li'l Tommy. The worker is spam.

The Clique

There was a small group consisting of the jocks and a few station staff members at WLS that became good friends. We eventually were the subject of a statement made by our beloved General Manager, Marty Greenberg. Marty was concerned that there appeared to be a clique within the station, and he wasn't sure he liked it. We felt we weren't hurting anyone, and we were the creative force at the radio station. So, it felt natural when we decided to call ourselves "The Clique." We would then quietly communicate any news of Clique Dinners, which would happen quite often. Actually, the Clique Dinners or Clique Parties began at our apartment while I was Program Director. At that time ratings were taken for several weeks four times a year. Mary Lou and I would have everyone over one night before a ratings period would start just to hang out, relax and eat good food. I felt it was a good time for everyone to bond. This continued after I stepped down from the PD job and went on for a few years.

Our apartment at that time had a closed-circuit television channel that featured a view of the building's lobby. Residents could see guests arriving and leaving. We had a tradition that everyone who left the party had to put on a skit in the lobby for the rest of us to enjoy. It was the proper way to say goodbye to everyone. After an evening of hanging out with good friends, food, beer, wine and shots of tequila, our guests lost some of their inhibitions when they would perform their goodbyes. As you can imagine there were many creative performances but the one I remember most starred JJ Jeffrey. There were a series of spotlights shining down on the lobby floor. JJ in his tattered wool coat with holes in the sleeves and a floppy hat would do his famous Jimmy Durante walk-off where he would stop under each spotlight, turn to the camera, tip his hat and wave to the rest of us. We not only enjoyed watching the creative way our friends would leave, but we also loved watching the reaction of Eddie the Doorman and other people in the lobby.

JJ Jeffrey had assigned nicknames for most of us and over time some of us came up with our own. Those that I remember are: John Landecker: "Decker;" Alan Rosen: "Mr. Al Lee;" Judy Mayer, who later became Judy Rosen after she married Mr. Al Lee: "Ms. Air Head;" Mary Lou: "Miss Lou;" John Gehron: "Geggins" because "Decker" couldn't remember John's name when he first met him and kept referring to him as "Geggins;" Elaine Hynson: "E-Dash;" Bob Sirott: "Rot;" Gil Gross: "Gilley;" Fred Winston: "Floyd;" Jim Smith: "Jukebox Jimmy or Box;" JJ Jeffrey: "Hole;" Ed Marcin: "Big Ed," Les Grobstein: "Grobber," Larry Lujack called himself "Ludge" and everyone called me: "T," and Fred Winston sometimes called me "Li'l Tony."

If you listened to WLS in the '70s, then you heard Ms. Air-Head's laugh. Judy Mayer Rosen has the funniest laugh and we used it in promos whenever we could. We called it "The Head Laugh."

Beginning in 1975, the Clique would meet at a WLS salesman's apartment on State Street – the same building we lived in – to watch Saturday Night Live (SNL) together. The WLS salesman was Simon T. He never used his last name. He was always just known as Simon T. Everyone would be sitting on the floor along with Simon's roommate – a Playboy Bunny – and his trained Doberman dog named Duke. We were there for the very first broadcast of SNL and no matter what our plans were on future Saturday nights, we would all wind up at Simon T's apartment around 10:30 p.m. It was a Clique tradition.

Then there was the wedding of a WLS staff member. She worked at the radio station as an assistant in the music department. She was well liked by everyone. The wedding was beautiful and then we all went to the reception nearby. However, we discovered a minor problem when we got there. The bartenders hadn't arrived yet. We all waited and after a half-hour or so, something had to be done; everyone was getting impatient. Scott Zolke, the Animal Stories attorney, and I jumped behind the bar and started serving drinks. Scott put a couple of dollars in a glass and we were in business. We found the beer on ice and the spirits were all there, so we did our best to provide refreshments to the whole group. On a few occasions people asked me to make a cocktail I was unfamiliar with, so I asked them what the ingredients were, and I put them on the bar and let the person make it themselves. We were very popular. Once the bartenders arrived it was obvious, they were NOT appreciative of our efforts to cover for them, so we rejoined the wedding party after reminding the bartenders they were about an hour late to their job.

The major promotion we did at WLS was the *Musicradio Game*. It involved people sending in their name, address and phone number on a postcard and I, along with production engineer Al Rosen, would call them on the telephone. First, I would tell them they were about to be recorded for radio broadcast. If they didn't object, we'd start the tape machine and I would ask them to say "hello" again as if they just answered the phone. Now after an edit it sounded like the phone rang, they answered, and I would ask "Is this (their name)?" They would say "yes", and I would ask

"What's your favorite radio station?" If they answered "WLS," I would award them whatever prize we were giving away. The prize, as I've mentioned before, would be anything from a new record album release to concert tickets, a sailboat, $1,000 cash, a digital watch, a trip to Walt Disney World and even a new car! It was a huge long-lasting promotion that went on for years.

The phone lines we used were shared with lines in the WLS Newsroom. Whenever the news people made an outgoing call, Rosen and I could hear them in our small studio in the back of the radio station. This made it easy for us to pull off a prank. During one of those outgoing calls, we heard one of our newsmen, Jeff Hendrix calling the Chicago Bears office to get a reaction from the team's management regarding their first-round draft pick that year: Wally Chambers. When we heard the person at the Bears' office put Jeff's call on hold, I picked up the phone in our small studio. I had to disguise my voice somewhat – so Jeff wouldn't know it was me – and I said, "Peacock." Jeff said, "Who is this?" I answered, "Ted Peacock – who is this?" Jeff identified himself and said he was looking to record a Bears representative's reaction to drafting Wally Chambers. I said, "Chalmbers – not Chambers." Jeff said, "Huh? His name is Chalmbers?" And I said, "Yes – don't call him Chambers. He hates that." Just then I heard a click and I realized a Bears executive had picked up his phone and I quietly hung up. Meanwhile, Rosen was laughing so hard, he ducked down under the table so he wouldn't break me up. We then heard Jeff tell the executive that he was just talking to Ted Peacock about Wally Chalmbers. The executive said, "What? Who is Ted Peacock and who is Wally Chalmbers?" Well, at this point Rosen and I were laughing ourselves silly and Jeff was stumbling around totally confused. He eventually got someone to give him a sound bite he could use in a newscast and hung up. Meanwhile, Rosen and I took a very low profile so the news department wouldn't figure out who Ted Peacock really was.

The 89ers

Over the years WLS raised hundreds of thousands of dollars and awareness for various charitable groups. We did a multi-day Radiothon to encourage listeners to give blood in 1973. Charlie Van Dyke originated the idea and he stayed on the air with other WLS air talent for 28 hours to assist the Chicago Red Cross. Lily Tomlin stopped by our studios and went on the air with Charlie. Later Lily asked Al Rosen, "Colonel" Karl Davis and me to help her put together an audio track from our vast sound-effect library for her standup act. It was fun working with her.

We started a basketball and softball team to raise money for school projects and/or families in need. We called ourselves "The WLS 89ers."

Our softball team was started by Bob Sirott. Sports reporter Les Grobstein, news anchor Harley Carnes and jocks John Landecker, Larry Lujack and Jeff Davis were initially on the team. I eventually joined the team and over time some of the guys dropped out. Sure, we had some ringers who were excellent ball players, but they were also good friends of the radio station. On occasion, Dennis DeYoung from the rock group Styx would play right field. Scott Zolke would play center field and other members of the WLS Staff would fill the roster.

We played one game against Billy Joel and his road crew. Billy wanted his team to be identified as Chico and the Crabs in that game. And after it was over Joel hosted a private party at a nearby tavern and paid for everything. We also had a softball game with the members of Journey that drew a big crowd. Unfortunately, they were disappointed that Steve Perry didn't show up.

There was an annual game each summer with members of the Chicago Blackhawks. These guys loved to play softball and they loved to party afterward. They were always very generous and cordial to us and our families.

Scott Zolke grew up in the Chicago Area but was working in Atlanta at that time. He would fly to Chicago each weekend to play softball with the 89ers. We never found out why Zolke never wore a cup! During that time Scott became a very close friend to my whole family. There were many evenings Scott would join our friend Ed Marcin of the WLS Promotion Department, Mary Lou and me for a night out. We'd have dinner and drinks and things would get a little crazy more often than not. But fortunately, Mary Lou was there to keep us out of trouble.

Our basketball team featured Larry Lujack, Les Grobstein, John Landecker, Jeff Hendrix and me from the air talent. It also included several other friends and staff members including a new Music Director Steve Perun whose nickname was "Pookie." I remember when Landecker complained about the colors of the WLS uniforms one year. He said they were the colors of Ohio State University and he would only wear colors of the University of Michigan. He was in maize and blue while the rest of the team was in grey and scarlet.

Once in a while, former Chicago Bulls guard John Mengelt coached the team and those games were pretty funny. He'd be very competitive and Lujack was usually busy smoking a cigarette during half time and ignoring Mengelt. In one game versus some ringers, we were down 30 points at half time so Mengelt put on his basketball shoes and single-handedly won the game for us. He scored something like 50 points in a short period of time while we just watched.

We had an extremely close game at Riverside Brookfield High School one night. The faculty had just scored and the 89ers were down by one point with only two seconds left in the game. I called a time out. In the huddle, we decided our 6-foot 8-inch center Ed Marcin would go stand right in front of the opposite basket. We needed someone who could pass the ball all the way down the court to Marcin so he could catch it and turn around and make the winning basket. WLS Newsman Jeff Hendrix said he could pass the ball that far, so we left it up to him. Hendrix took the position behind the opposite baseline and passed the ball to Marcin. Instead, the ball sailed over Marcin's head, zoomed over the backboard and hit the big scoreboard up on the wall and we lost the game. We all burst out laughing. At least Hendrix was right. He could pass it that far!

Larry always had an escape plan after every game. A big crowd would gather to get his autograph. Each time, Larry would throw up a handful of his wallet-size publicity pictures and as the crowd scrambled to pick them up, Larry and his wife Jude would hit the exit.

After 89ers baseball and basketball games, we all went to nearby restaurants for pizza and beer. The children of the team always enjoyed having their own space with soft drinks and pizza. On one occasion we all arrived at a pizzeria and mentioned to the owner of the small restaurant that we were there to help. I took over the host job and when other customers arrived, I'd call up to Ed, Scott and one or two other team members that a party of 3 or 4 needed a table. They would scout for one available and even bus a table to prepare it for future use. The owner of the pizzeria was enjoying what we were doing, and we told him we wouldn't handle any money, just seating people and busing tables until our food was ready.

Other customers at the restaurant were enjoying what was going on around them and some wanted to pitch in. Mary Lou's parents were visiting from Virginia and they were having so much fun they thought about extending their stay another week to go out with the team again. It was a fun evening and the owner told us we were welcome to return anytime.

Larry only joined us for beer and pizza once that I can remember. That was after a harness racing appearance where we all dressed in jockey gear and participated in the Celebrity Feature Race. I can't recall who won but I do remember on the last turn Larry's horse took off running to the barn despite him yelling at it and trying to get it back on the track. He told me later that on that turn, his horse passed gas and headed straight for the barn. I burst out laughing and said that we will have to cover what happened in the next *Animal Stories* broadcast. Even when he told the story on-the-air, I burst out laughing again because I could still hear him yelling and trying to turn his horse with no luck. I told him it sounded like a nightmare. "It WAS a nightmare, Lil Tommy."

After the race we, along with our families, all went to a private room at a restaurant for dinner. Larry said he would prefer to sit at the children's table so he could "rap with the kids." During dinner, our eight-year-old daughter Shannon came to the adult table and complained, "Larry isn't talking to us." We all laughed! I told her to keep trying.

Our biggest basketball game was on an extremely cold night in Morris, Illinois – a town about an hour's drive southwest of Chicago. This story begins with an *Animal Stories* broadcast several weeks earlier. In the *Animal Stories* report, Uncle Lar' read a story about a Morris Policeman cornering a raccoon in a garage and reportedly opening fire with his service revolver to kill it. As usual Lar' embellished the story painting a picture of a helpless little critter coming in contact with this really tough guy – a heavily armed "pole leese" dude with guns blasting on anything that moved as he entered the garage. Soon after that *Animal Stories* report, we received an invitation from the Morris Police to come and settle this thing on the basketball court. Larry and I kept this issue alive on the air and accepted the invitation while stoking the competition saying they had better be ready for an embarrassing outcome. Off the air our promotion department worked closely with the police department to arrange a game to raise funds for the Grundy County United Fund. The cops were more than kind and supportive. They had arranged motel rooms for us and our families. A huge "Welcome WLS" was displayed on the motel sign. Police personnel invited several of us to tour their offices and during that time, I was locked in a jail cell for several minutes. I was hoping it was a joke. It was. They arranged a private postgame party for the officers and their families along with the 89ers and our families. There was an even bigger party for the game's ticket holders. The police arranged to transport us from the motel to the school and when we arrived, we were shocked at the number of people lined up in the bitter cold waiting to get in. As a result, the gym was packed. The mayor of Morris tossed up the ceremonial jump ball.

The game was sponsored by the Morris *Daily Herald*. The newspaper's edition of February 1, 1982 had extensive coverage of the game along with great photos. According to the Herald, Larry shot two for seventeen from the floor and three for eight from the free throw line. He ended up with seven points for the game. WLS's Les Grobstein reported on the air that so far for the season, Larry had shot three for thirty-two. In a post-game interview with the Herald's Sports Editor Bob Black, Larry said he was a "runner and gunner and famous for his behind the back passes." I didn't do any better. I ended with seven points which I think was a career high. Les Grobstein scored three points. Thank goodness for a member of the WLS Sales staff, Jerry Ryan who ended with thirteen points and Biff Fanslow from the WLS Commissary who scored ten. The police department called the first time out of the game and Larry went out to center court and did a cheer with the high school cheerleaders. The crowd loved it and the rest of the team didn't let him forget it. The final score was WLS 89ers 68 – the Fraternal Order of Police (Lodge 79) 47.

And maybe for full disclosure, I should mention that Biff Fanslow didn't really work for the WLS Commissary since there was no such department. We introduced him that way to give him a title. He was really a good friend of Ed Marcin and the rest of WLS staff and a good ballplayer we welcomed to the team!

Someone was smart enough to bring a video camera to the game to record this epic event. I don't know whatever happened to the tape. Brant Miller, his wife Lisa Miller, Mary Lou and Jude Lujack provided some very creative and funny play-by-play.

After the game and the public party, there was yet another private party at a police officer's home. One member of our team was invited to join the host in the backyard shooting guns at some old tires. We drove home the next morning in a snowstorm, but we thanked the whole community for their hospitality.

We were fortunate to have many other games that were sold-out. One of those was a basketball game where we teamed up with players of the Chicago Bears including the late Walter Payton. According to Jim O'Donnell's column in Suburban Chicago's *The Daily Herald* of March 27, 1981, leading up to the game, other Bears players would include Doug Plank, Ted Albrecht, Len Waltersheid, Gary Campbell and Dan Neal (but no Wally Chalmbers). The opposing team was made up of area high school basketball coaches, many of whom were stars while they were in college. Our team did have a ringer – Creighton University star, Kevin McKenna. The game was played at Rolling Meadows High School and was a fundraiser for a local charity. I can't recall who won the game, but I do remember in the locker room we all were exhausted. But Walter Payton said he wanted to go and run a few miles before he showered. So he went out to the school's track and by the time he returned we had all left. The other Bears players said they weren't surprised that Walter wanted to do more because he was in incredible shape.

In most cases we played against teams made up of police and fire departments or school faculties. And in most cases, we usually lost.

Ed Marcin of the WLS Promotion Department was the point person at the radio station for most of these events. Ed made sure everyone knew all the details of each game. He also contacted his counterparts of each event for follow up. He made many good friends which made the events even more successful. Some of those friendships are still strong today. The success of our softball and basketball games was due in large part to "Big Ed."

There were other opportunities to meet listeners on behalf of the radio station in the form of personal appearances. These events were usually arranged through clients of the station in order to draw listeners to their retail locations. Some record executives asked for disc jockeys to be involved in a stunt or event that drew attention to new albums being released. On one occasion the radio station asked me to do my show aboard a hot air balloon to promote a new movie and its soundtrack album. When I arrived at the location of the broadcast, the weather wasn't cooperating. The skies were cloudy and there was a possibility of rain. But the clients assured me that I would be able to go up in the balloon to do the show and if there was lightning in the area, they'd land and I'd be safe. Furthermore, the hot air balloon basket would be tethered so I wouldn't be up in the air with no way to land. I went up and about an hour and a half into my four-hour show, the first flash of lightning occurred very close to me in the balloon. Maybe it was several hundred yards away from me, but it sure felt and sounded like it was way too close! The handlers grabbed the tether rope and pulled me down to the ground. They couldn't get me down fast enough!

Another time I was asked to do my show from the Goodyear Blimp. That was a special treat because I often wondered what it would be like to be in that kind of airship. *Chicago Sun-Times* reporter Robert Feder wrote in his June 15, 1984 column that I had mentioned to him one of the most famous broadcasts in WLS history: when Herb Morrison was an eyewitness to the Hindenburg crash at Lakehurst, New Jersey on May 6, 1937. A German passenger zeppelin caught fire and was destroyed killing 36 of the

97 people on board. I told him that I had almost forgotten about that and it made me a little nervous. The Goodyear Blimp isn't a zeppelin. It's filled with helium, not highly flammable hydrogen. I mentioned to Feder, "It sounds pretty safe and it's just another part of what we all have to go through to entertain the kids." When I climbed on-board that day it turned out to be a wonderful experience. The only problem I had was communicating with the air-studio. This was done long before cell phones and I had to use a primitive two-way radio hooked up to a phone that wasn't very reliable. I relaxed and enjoyed the ride.

Feder and I talked about other stunts I had been asked to do. I told him I drew the line when it came to sitting on an elephant. I said, "I've been asked to, but I've heard too many horror stories about what can happen. So, I've never done it." I was asked to play Donkey Basketball a few times earlier in my career in Topeka. I hated it because the donkeys wouldn't move, and I fell off more than once.

There were parades too, like the St. Patrick's Day parade which was always fun. On-air Lujack would describe the drunk teenagers waving and shouting at us to throw souvenirs to the crowd. We had quite a memorable night when we appeared in the Venetian Night Parade of Boats along the lakefront. First, we had a predicament with some Frisbees. We tried tossing them into the crowd only to see them land in the lake, causing people to dive in after them. One of them actually flew into a private party and landed in the middle of the buffet table, causing food to fly everywhere. Authorities have since prohibited this type of thing and for good reason. That same night the yacht we rented went out on the lake after the parade just in time for a thunderstorm. We were all below deck enjoying food and drinks and some of us were turning green. Before we reached the dock, many of us were hanging over the rail of the boat and you can imagine we laughed about that days later.

While most of us loved being in the parades, Lujack really didn't like them. When a major brewing company asked the *Animal Stories* News Team to ride on their float, Lar – wearing his cowboy hat – sat still, looking straight ahead the whole time. Fans were waving and I was waving back but Lar' just sat still. We approached the official reviewing stand where Mayor Jane Byrne was sitting with various city dignitaries and Larry asked me to tell him when they were looking at us. When I cued him, he turned quickly, waved at the group and returned to looking straight ahead.

WLS did a large number of remote broadcasts from Great America in Gurnee, Illinois when it first opened. We were always in Hometown Square and it was a time when we all took turns doing live commercials and playing the music as loud as we could. Over time we had a VIP room set up for us, so our families had a place to relax privately. It was on the second floor of one of the vendor locations in the park. There were soft drinks and sandwiches provided and we usually had the two rooms to ourselves.

On one occasion we graciously gave up the larger of the two rooms to the rock group Survivor. They kept the door between the two rooms closed and locked. That wasn't a big issue EXCEPT the only way to get to the VIP bathroom was through the Survivor room. The band had played a pre-event concert in the Great America parking lot. Most of the WLS staff had children who needed to use the bathroom and the guys in the band didn't want us to walk through their room. Well, they eventually backed off and our kids were allowed to get to the bathroom without a problem.

You can imagine how we handled this on the air the following Monday! We used humor but the message was clear – the band who played the parking lot wouldn't allow the little kids to use the bathroom. A few days after the Great America event, Survivor had a child's potty chair delivered to the radio station with a card signed by the band! All was forgiven.

Everyone in radio will tell you that personal appearances are all part of the job. But for us, in everything we did we were just having fun and feeling like we were doing some good for our listeners. It was a time I will never forget.

Look Who Showed Up!

There was no shortage of celebrities visiting the WLS Musicradio studios. How about some name dropping: We all enjoyed discovering Steve Perry outside the viewing window of the air studio holding a sign saying "Play more Journey." Judy Collins spent her 40th birthday at WLS promoting her latest album, *Hard Time for Lovers*. I remember the cover of her album caused a lot of talk because it featured a nude photo of Judy. She told me she was very proud of the cover and her message was, "I'm 40 years old and I've still got it." Rodney Dangerfield spent an hour with me prior to filming a television commercial for Larry Lujack's show. He kept me laughing with his one-liners. We had lived in the same neighborhood back in New York and I'd see him often on the street. John Travolta sat in during my show promoting his new movie *Grease* in 1978. The photo that was taken of the two of us in the studio hung in my home office. Mary Lou says it always got the biggest reaction from the teenage babysitters in the neighborhood. A few years later I met John's sister, Ellen, when we did a radio commercial together. Jim Belushi and Dan Aykroyd spent time with John Landecker one evening while they were filming *The Blues Brothers*. Bette Midler joined me on the air for an hour talking about her movie *The Rose*. Tanya Tucker and her father Beau Tucker were in the studio for a *MusicPeople* interview. They were very excited to meet "Colonel" Karl Davis. Tina Turner was interviewed by Yvonne Daniels. I jumped at the chance to have a photo taken with both ladies. Art Garfunkel was another star very impressed with meeting Karl Davis. I interviewed Olivia Newton-John in her hotel room. I was a little intimidated by the large staff surrounding her. She was very soft spoken and reserved but also very kind. I admit I was starstruck. One of my most embarrassing blunders was my interview with Eddie Kendricks of Motown. I began the interview with "Tonight on *MusicPeople* our guest is the former lead singer of the Temptations, Eddie Hendrix...." Eddie interrupted me saying, "Hey man, my name is Kendricks, not Hendrix." Board-Op Al Rosen almost fell out of his chair laughing and I felt like a complete idiot. Fortunately, the program was not live. We stopped the tape and started over. It was obvious Eddie wasn't very comfortable for the rest of the interview. I didn't blame him. One day while walking down Michigan Avenue, I bumped into Lionel Richie. He greeted me with, "Hey, Li'l Tommy." One evening Jim Kerr, Mary Lou and I were invited to dinner with the Osmonds at the Ambassador East Hotel. It was a fun evening and we got to know how generous and kind the family is.

We Couldn't Have Done It Without Them

Along with the air-talent, we had a large number of people working behind the scenes that were a part of the radio station's success. I wish I could name everyone but it's not possible. Some of the people are mentioned in the various chapters of this book. Here are a few others: Cindy Gatzilois from the programming department went on to produce other radio air-talent and was highly respected and much loved. Cindy passed away in 2014 and there was a large group of WLS alums at her wake. Mickey Gillogly Nelson was the Executive Secretary to Marty Greenberg. She formed a musical group "Mickey & the Memories" who performed throughout the area. She is also involved in the Chicago Cultural Center's program of recreating old-time-radio shows live on-stage. She directed a performance of a *Sam Spade* detective show starring National Radio Hall of Famer John Landecker in the title role.

I sat in the audience and enjoyed every minute of it and marveled how much work the cast and crew, including sound effect artists, put into the show. Linda Waldman from the WLS Promotion Department is a very gifted artist. Her drawings and paintings are exceptional. Karen Esken of the WLS Promotion Department went on to be an executive in the Disney organization. Bev Black was the long time Traffic Director programming the commercials content. Brant Miller became a television weatherman at NBC Channel 5 in Chicago. Linda Marshall and Catherine Johns were two of the outstanding news people. Jack Swanson was another news person who went on to be an extremely successful news executive in San Francisco. Pam Murphy and Elaine Hynson were two outstanding board operators. Don Bouloukos was a WLS salesperson who eventually went on to be a senior executive with CBS Radio. Ed Marcin of the WLS Promotion Department is Vice President of Public Affairs & Special Projects at Clear Channel Outdoor in Chicago. Jerry Ryan, another sales executive went on to become a senior executive of Hispanic radio companies.

Eventually, everyone moved on because of career changes. I've always felt the staff of those WLS Musicradio Days was made up of very special people. In the many years I worked with them, I realized the success we had was due to the collaboration of everyone that worked there. It was every department and every individual who worked tirelessly in making the radio station great.

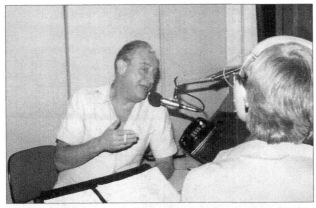

CHAPTER 8

And Now...the Chicago Bulls

"Sirius – Eye in the Sky" – Alan Parsons Project
"Rock-n-Roll Part II" – Gary Glitter
"What I Like About You" – The Romantics

BEFORE I BEGAN WORKING AS PUBLIC ADDRESS Announcer for the Chicago Bulls, I was a fan. I had been to several Bulls games before. Back in those days, it was never a problem getting a ticket. They were never sold out. One day in 1976 the General Sales Manager of WLS, Joe Parish, asked me to drop by his office after I finished my air-shift. He asked on behalf of a friend in the Bulls organization if I'd be interested in doing some announcing at Chicago Bulls games. I told Joe I was indeed interested. He gave me the contact information and I arranged to meet with their marketing people led by Mike McClure. The business office of the Bulls was located across Michigan Avenue from the radio station.

During the meeting, I was offered a salary per game and I could park in the lot across the street from the Chicago Stadium for free. I couldn't believe it. They wanted to pay me to attend Bulls games. Of course, I said yes!

My first season was very exciting. It was the year the American Basketball Association (ABA) merged with the National Basketball Association (NBA) and players from the ABA were drafted by NBA teams. The Bulls picked 7' 2" center Artis Gilmore from the Kentucky Colonels of the ABA. Other players on the team were Jerry Sloan, Norm Van Lier, Wilbur Holland, Tom Boerwinkle, Phil Hicks, Bob Love, Cliff Pondexter, John Mengelt, first-round draft pick Scott May from Indiana and a few others. The head coach was former assistant coach Ed Badger.

The music during the games was supplied by Nancy Faust – the organist for the Chicago White Sox – who played a portable organ that was brought into the stadium for each game. She always played just the right music at just the right time in the game. If the fans didn't like a call against the Bulls, she would go into "Three Blind Mice" just to have fun with the refs. Benny the Bull is the team mascot. He was named after the first Bulls stadium announcer Ben Bentley, and Benny has been a crowd favorite since 1969. Recently Benny was inducted into the Mascot Hall of Fame. The only other entertainment at the time was a heavy-set fellow who wore a T-shirt that identified himself as "Superfan." During some of the time-outs he would run around the stadium waving a towel while Nancy was playing some fast music and I would call out, "Where are you, Superfan?"

Jim Durham was the play-by-play radio announcer for the Bulls on radio station WIND. He worked solo for a few years and eventually teamed up with former player Norm Van Lier, talk-radio host Dave Baum and eventually with Johnny "Red" Kerr. Jim Durham was, in my opinion, the best play by play announcer in the NBA at that time. He was the recipient of the Basketball Hall of Fame 2011 Curt Goody Media Award. Johnny Kerr, a member of the Illinois Athletics Hall of Fame, was the original head coach of the Bulls in 1966 but before that, he was a star at the University of Illinois and played professional ball with the Syracuse Nationals of the ABA.

The Bulls had a terrific season during my first year with the team. They made the playoffs and faced the team that would eventually win the NBA Championship that season: The Portland Trailblazers. That was the first of many great years of sitting midcourt and getting paid for it.

In my early days, the Stadium would rarely be anything close to a full house. In some cases, the Stadium wouldn't even open some of the higher levels of seats and occasionally on some cold, snowy nights I was asked to make announcements to encourage fans to "come down closer to the court and enjoy the game and make sure you pick up a free ticket to an upcoming game on your way out."

When the Bulls started a long string of home victories in my first season, the Stadium started rockin' because the crowds got to be huge! The largest crowd my first year was one of the last games of the regular season. It was against the Houston Rockets with over 18,000 people. The average crowd for Bulls games in the 1976-1977 season was just over 11,600. And the one playoff game at the Chicago Stadium versus Portland was sold out and hosted the loudest crowd of the entire season. Wow! Things have really gotten bigger and better. In the 2017-2018 season, the Bulls led the entire League in attendance – averaging 20,776 fans.

After a few years, the Bulls' game management invited me to a meeting in the offseason and said they would like to have popular music played during the games. I told them I loved the idea. I helped them design a production unit consisting of two radio station cart machines, a microphone, and a cassette player. I would dub songs onto carts from the radio station and play them during the games along with all of the regular announcing.

Most of my announcements would be whatever the officials called during the game, the time-outs and the team announcements about upcoming games. One of the first things I worked on was the introduction of the starting lineup. I always wanted to make the starting lineup introduction very exciting and special. Now I was able to do that because I could use popular music. In the first few years, I used the theme of the *Miami Vice* TV show, "Thriller" by Michael Jackson and some other popular songs of the day. We also featured a lights-out introduction with a spotlight on the players as I introduced them.

During the most exciting moments of the games, I played "Rock n Roll Part II" by Gary Glitter. It didn't take long for other teams in the league to call the Bulls office and get my home phone number. They would ask, "What's that song you played?" It was always "Rock n Roll Part II." That recording became the most popular song at sporting events everywhere from that point on. I was the first to use it at a sporting event at Chicago Stadium. It is still used in college, high school and grade school athletic events.

In 1984, the Bulls had the 3rd pick in the first round of the collegiate draft and selected 21-year-old Michael Jordan from

North Carolina. Michael was also on the U.S. Olympic Team that year. While he was in Bulls training camp, I began hearing about this rookie who was dunking over the big guys. We all knew we were looking at a very exciting future for the Chicago Bulls. The team office called me at home and asked if I'd come up with a new and unique introduction for the starting lineup with Michael being the last player announced. I started thinking about what song I could use. I couldn't come up with anything I really liked.

One night Mary Lou and I attended a movie at the legendary Biograph Theatre in Chicago. Before the film started, there was contemporary background music playing in the theatre. I heard the song "Sirius" which is the introduction to the Alan Parsons Project song "Eye in the Sky." I leaned over to Mary Lou and said "I know this song. This would work for the Bulls intro." The next day I went out and bought the record, took it home and spent most of the afternoon listening to it over and over. I had my stopwatch and the Bulls lineup. I worked on the timing until I had what I liked. I called the Bulls office and said, "I think I found the song we're looking for." I asked Tom Schnecke – who was a board operator at WLS – to dub "Sirius" onto a cart and I practiced in the radio studio before I went to the Chicago Stadium for the next game. It was during that game that I used it for the first time and the Bulls management loved it. It didn't take long for the song "Sirius" to be heard everywhere in sporting events. I had it timed out. I started the introduction with, "Aaaaaannnnnd Now, The Starting Lineup for Your Chicago Bulls." I alternated using "in the middle" with "the man in the middle" when introducing the player in the center position of the team lineup. My eight-year-old daughter Amy told me on the way home from a game that she really liked hearing "the man in the middle". That sealed it for me. I've used it ever since.

In 1988 the NBA All-Star Game was played at Chicago Stadium. I had the opportunity to do all of the public address duties of the events. The slam dunk competition remains one of the most memorable contests. It all came down to future Hall of Famers Dominique Wilkins of the Atlanta Hawks and Michael Jordan of the Chicago Bulls. Dominique was a nine-time NBA All-Star. Michael won the competition on his home court and it was a thrilling event. The game itself the next day was special because of all the talent on the floor but it was obvious the players weren't interested in playing defense. The final score was 138-133 in favor of the East All-Stars. Michael Jordan was voted the Most Valuable Player, scoring 40 points with 8 rebounds and 4 blocked shots. Dominique was the second highest scorer on the East with 29 points. For the West, Karl Malone had 22 points and Hakeem Olajuwon had 21. I treasure a keepsake from that game – my own NBA All-Star ring with my name on the side.

There were some unusual and humorous events during my time with the Bulls at Chicago Stadium. The building itself was old – having opened in 1929 – and I recall former New York Knick and U.S. Senator Bill Bradley refer to the building in his 1976 book *Life on the Run* as "a relic from the past." In one instance NBA Hall of Famer Patrick Ewing of the New York Knicks was at the free-throw line about to shoot two free-throws. He bounced the ball a few times and was about to let the first shot fly when the stadium horn of the Chicago Blackhawks went off. This horn is actually a boat horn and incredibly loud. Ewing tossed the ball back to the referee and looked over at us with fire in his eyes. We at the scorer's table looked puzzled because we had no idea why it happened. The ref passed the ball back to Ewing who bounced the ball and was about ready to shoot when the boat horn sounded again! This time the referee came over to the table to ask what happened. In the meantime, one of the stadium electricians ran over and crawled under the scorer's table and found that Johnny Kerr had accidentally kicked a loose wire under the table which caused the horn to sound off.

In another incident, Darryl Dawkins of the Philadelphia 76ers came over to the table and sat in front of Bob Rosenberg, the head scorer, and me to check into the game. He had to wait until the next dead ball to get permission to enter the game, so we asked Darryl how he was doing. He began to ramble on about some things going on in his life. Pretty soon there was an out-of-bounds play causing the clock to stop and the horn sounded to get Darryl into the game. But he's still talking to us and Bob and I had to remind him he was needed on the floor to play.

In March of 1990, I resigned from the Bulls because I had accepted a job with CBS Radio to program WODS-FM in Boston. My last game was against the Phoenix Suns and during the pre-game, I was given a beautiful inscribed watch along with a Bulls Jersey and great applause from the fans. I stood at center court and did the Bulls starting lineup with the players all coming out and shaking my hand. It was a memorable night!

Over the next few years, I received calls from the Bulls asking me if I'd consider returning as the public address announcer. I always told them I loved doing it at the time, but my first profession was radio and that meant I had to go where the job was and, in this case, it was Boston. Two years later it was Los Angeles. As

Mary Lou used to say, "If you want to see the country, marry a guy who works in radio."

I was living in both Boston and Los Angeles when the Bulls won their 6 NBA Championships. I never lost my passion for the Chicago Bulls. I cheered them to every victory no matter where I was living. But I always wished I was there courtside experiencing the thrill of winning. The Bulls have always been very gracious and generous– even to the point of sending me NBA Championship watches and a jewelry box with my name inscribed.

In the fall of 2003, my radio career returned the family to Chicago. A short time later I received a call from Steve Schanwald, VP of Operations for the Bulls. Steve and I had worked together during my early years with the team. Steve Scott, who was doing the PA at the time, was leaving for a new radio job in New York. Steve Schanwald asked if I'd be interested in returning to the Bulls who, by this time, were playing at the United Center. I said yes, returned to the Bulls courtside and remained with the team until late 2019. I'm very proud to have been a part of this organization for more than 25 seasons.

Game entertainment has improved tremendously over the last several years. Game hosts were added to the mix introducing acts from the floor and in the crowd. Half time entertainment features contemporary musical artists and young people in a youth talent search. We had a visual artist who painted an image set to rock music. The painting was auctioned off to raise money for Chicago Bulls Charities. Daredevil acts and skilled balancing performers are just a few of the wide variety of family-oriented features. The Bulls Kids are outstanding young people who are incredible dancers! The Swingin' Seniors are mature ladies who have choreographers that teach them the latest dance moves from Chicago's best nightclubs. The extremely talented Luvabulls are a troop of women dancers who – along with Benny the Bull – are the perfect ambassadors of the Bulls Organization. When fans come to a game, they find performers all around the concourse on various levels, and everyone is entertained from the moment they enter the United Center. New team introduction visuals were added with lights, music and even projections on the playing surface. Videos run pre-anthem, showing the sights of Chicago from many landmarks and neighborhoods while Frank Sinatra sings "Chicago." Then a historical video set to music features images of players and coaches over the previous 50+ seasons showcasing the pride of Chicago's basketball heritage. And of course, we use "Sirius" to introduce the starting lineup of the Bulls players.

During the 2015-2016 season, we learned the NBA Champion Golden State Warriors were using "Sirius" to introduce their starting lineup. *The Wall Street Journal* ran a story mentioning players on that team who said they grew up hearing that music while Michael Jordan was leading the Bulls to six NBA Championships and they wanted it too. The Journal contacted me to include the history behind that music of how and when I first introduced it to the game.

That iconic introduction became popular in sporting events around the country and places you might not expect. In 2009 Oprah Winfrey's staff invited me to make an appearance on her television show to recreate the introduction for the starting lineup of contestants in a cake baking competition. A few months later they contacted me again to do a special introduction for her secret guest in a prime-time television broadcast who turned out to be: Michael Jordan.

And there were weddings. I was asked by dozens of brides and grooms to do a starting lineup announcement of their bridal party. These turned out to be fun because of the creative writing that the couples put into the scripts.

My job kept me very busy from pre-game until post-game. I arrived no later than 3 hours before tip-off for rehearsal. I made all of the announcements during the hour leading up to game time. During the game, I made all announcements of rulings on the court by the officials. I kept track of and announced personal fouls, team fouls, substitutions, players who scored, players who were attempting free throws, team time outs and of course, promotional announcements during the time outs. There were announcements after the final buzzer of post-game interviews, fan rewards and the next home game.

My son Tommy was lucky enough to be a ball-boy for nine seasons. He and the other ball-boys rebounded during warm-ups, mopped up any moisture from perspiration on the court, laundered the towels after the game and countless other jobs. Tommy also was asked by a visiting assistant coach to help him and superstar Kevin Durant work on post moves by passing the ball to Durant during the pre-game shoot-around. Tommy has told me the NBA players are always courteous to the ball boys and appreciate all the hard work they do.

In almost three decades of working for the Chicago Bulls, Mary Lou and I have made many friends. We got to know the late Norm Van Lier before I started working with the team. He was a neighbor of ours. We all lived in the same high rise in downtown Chicago. Hall of Famer Scottie Pippen is a former player we enjoy spending time talking to. John and Linda Mengelt have been close friends for over 40 years. Mary Lou and I are godparents to their daughter, Jennifer. The late Tom Boerwinkle and his wife Linda, John and Carolyn Paxson and Doug Collins are all friends along with several longtime Chicago Bulls staff employees.

In late 2019 I retired as the Public Address Announcer. My last game was November 9th, versus the Houston Rockets. It was a night I'll never forget.

When I introduced the starting lineup, each player came over to the scorers' table to give me a fist bump. Two of the players on the Rockets who were once with the Bulls also came over to congratulate me. The Bulls produced a tribute video that ran during a time out in the first quarter. It chronicled my time with the team with highlights of innovations that I introduced. The crowd gave me a standing ovation. I was stunned and honored by the work that went in to making the video. Mary Lou and Tommy were there courtside to share the love. I didn't know it then but in the fourth quarter, the United Center television camera spent most of the time on me doing my job. After the game Michael Reinsdorf, President and COO of the Bulls, came over to the table. I had the chance to shake his hand and thank him for his support. He told me he remembers being an 11-year-old kid coming to a game with his father and hearing me introduce "Mickeeeeey Johnson." I also had the opportunity to thank Michelle McComas, Senior Director of Entertainment and Events, for arranging a special night I'll always remember.

There isn't a time I don't feel grateful for the Chicago Bulls experience I've lived.

CHAPTER 9

Keep It Moving, Daahling

"Superbowl Shuffle" – Chicago Bears
"California Dreamin" – Mamas & Papas
"Time of the Season" – The Zombies

THE WJMK CALL LETTERS HAVE A SPECIAL MEANING to me and you will soon understand why. The station originally signed on in 1948 as WCFL-FM. In 1961 it became WJJD-FM. At some point they changed the call letters to WJEZ to go along with a country format. Infinity Broadcasting acquired the station in 1983 and a year later they adopted an oldies format and became WJMK. I was told the letters "MK" of WJMK supposedly referred to Mel Karmazin who was then President of Infinity Broadcasting.

I left WLS when my contract expired at the end of November 1985. WLS had offered me a 10-year contract to work with Larry. They didn't make much of an effort to sell me on the proposal so I turned it down.

I had a great run at WLS, but I decided it was time to move on. I wanted to take the entire month of December off and I turned down some offers to talk during that month with two other Chicago radio stations. I just needed a break. I was at the point I really didn't know what I wanted to do next.

In early January 1986 I was invited to New York City to meet with WCBS-FM's Program Director Joe McCoy about joining the air-staff. Joe and I worked together at WOR-FM in the early 70's and we are still good friends. Unfortunately, it didn't work out. It wasn't the right move for me and my family at that time. I also met CBS-FM's General Manager Nancy Widman who later became President of CBS Radio. I later worked for Nancy as Program Director of CBS stations in Boston and Los Angeles.

Terry Rodda, a former WLS Research Analyst was now the General Manager of a radio station in San Antonio. He called and asked if I was interested in a programming position there. After giving it some serious thought, I decided that it was best to stay in Chicago.

The next call came from Harvey Pearlman, General Manager of WJMK. The station was also known as Magic 104. He told me their morning man, the legendary Joel Sebastian, was in the hospital and I should "get off my ass and have some fun playing some great music in the morning until he returns."

I agreed to the temporary position. I didn't intend on making this permanent. This was going to be a fun job and I loved oldies music, so I joined the talent lineup just in time to get involved in a promotion in conjunction with the Chicago Bears going to Super Bowl XX vs the New England Patriots.

WJMK came up with an on-air promotion with the Infinity station WBCN-FM in Boston about the two teams in the Super

Bowl. Boston morning man Charles Laquadera and I would connect by phone each morning leading up to the game and chide each other live on the air about what team would win. The phone wasn't the only way we could connect. There was a special line WBCN and Magic 104 shared so listeners in Boston and Chicago could actually hear each other's broadcast anytime we turned it on. Of course, we made a bet on the game. He decided if the Patriots won the game, he wanted me to send Chicago deep dish pizzas and steaks. I decided that if the Bears won, I wanted live lobsters and a Patriot tri-corner hat. I asked him if his radio station had a flagpole and he said they did. So, I said along with the lobsters and the hat I want you to fly a Chicago Bears flag on your flagpole for a couple of weeks. He agreed. We kept the friendly rivalry going on until game day.

The Bears did win the Super Bowl, beating New England 46-10. In a few days I got my tri-corner Patriot hat which was too small, and a dozen live lobsters had arrived separately to the WJMK studios one afternoon. By the time I came to work the next morning, the lobsters were all gone. The best thing to come out of the bet was that the Chicago Bears sent WBCN a Bears Flag to fly on their flagpole. I was told the station flew the Bears flag for a couple of weeks. I should have asked for photo proof!

About a week before the Super Bowl and while I was on the air, I received a call in the studio from Joel Sebastian's son Mark, who told me that his dad had passed away. I announced this terribly sad news on the air. Joel was a much-loved radio talent in Chicago having worked at WLS, WGN, WMAQ and WCFL before WJMK. He was only 53 years old. Before working in Chicago, Joel worked in Dallas, Detroit and Los Angeles. When my show ended that morning, I met with General Manager Harvey Pearlman who said that my job was now permanent. I said I wasn't sure I wanted that. That's not what I originally agreed to. This was just a fun temporary job until Joel could come back. Besides, by this time I knew what I wanted. I wanted to get into a program director's job again and WJMK already had an excellent PD, Gary Price. I didn't want to make any commitments to stay on the morning show.

Not long after the Super Bowl, G. Michael Donovan, the General Manager of WKQX-FM called me. At that time WKQX-FM was owned by NBC. He asked if I'd be interested in programming that Adult Contemporary formatted station. G. Michael and I worked together at WLS for several years. He was the promotion director when I first arrived at WLS and later he worked in the sales department. I met with Donovan and decided to accept the position of Program Director of WKQX also known as Q101 and said goodbye to my friends at Magic 104. I didn't know it then, but I would return to WJMK two more times in my career.

WKQX's studios were located in the huge Merchandise Mart along the Chicago River. The building is enormous, having 4 million square feet of floor space. It was the largest building in the world when it opened in 1930. In 1986 it housed both WKQX and WMAQ radio and Channel 5 WMAQ-TV. All of these properties were owned by the National Broadcasting Company.

WKQX was already a successful radio station when I took over the programming. The air staff consisted of very talented people including the morning show with Robert Murphy, Beth Kaye, Pete Stacker, Dave McBride and Pat Benkowski. Greg Brown and Dan Walker were the midday and afternoon air-talent respectively. A great lineup.

144

I would travel to NBC Headquarters in New York on occasion for corporate meetings at 30 Rockefeller Center. I enjoyed working with my counterparts at other NBC owned stations and it provided me with a number of valuable contacts.

One of my favorite promotions was a contest to have listeners join our morning show on a weekend trip to New York to attend *Saturday Night Live.* Then they would have a free day on Sunday to explore the city and be in the audience to see *Late Night with David Letterman* on Monday evening. Letterman came out to talk to the audience before the show and wound up talking to one of our listeners. She told Letterman she won tickets to the show on a Chicago radio station. Letterman smiled, chuckled and asked "What was first prize?"

Both television shows were on NBC. Our morning team was broadcasting their show from the NBC Radio Network Studios in Rockefeller Center with special guests from Chicago including Gene Siskel and Roger Ebert who were in New York at the time. Former WMAQ-TV news anchor Jane Pauly was also a guest.

The Promotion Director of Q101 was Gloria Hinrichs. Gloria created a promotion that could only happen once in 75 years! We took listeners to a beautiful resort in Puerto Rico to witness Halley's Comet when it was visible from Earth in 1986. Puerto Rico was the ideal place to see this spectacular event. The *Murphy in the Morning* show was broadcast live, poolside, at the resort that week. One special night we all went out on the golf course far away from the lights and witnessed that unforgettable sight.

While I was at WKQX, the General Electric Company bought NBC and new management came into Chicago about the time a major union contract was expiring at WMAQ, WKQX and

WMAQ-TV. GE officials told us that they didn't think negotiations were going to go well. Furthermore, we should be prepared for a work stoppage of engineering and board operators at the radio stations and camera operators and others at the television station. The strike did happen and everyone in management had dual responsibilities of doing their normal radio duties and helping out at the television station. I was fortunate that I never had to cross the picket line to do a union job as I was too busy with the programming duties. The strike lasted several months and those pulling double duty received a bonus in the form of General Electric stock.

I was at WKQX for a couple of years and still doing my public address duties with the Chicago Bulls. One day I got a call from WJMK General Manager Harvey Pearlman who invited me to lunch. I had a feeling I knew what was coming.

At an Italian restaurant on Michigan Avenue, Pearlman asked me to come back to WJMK to do the morning show. He offered me a very large salary. After talking it over with Mary Lou, I agreed to the terms and resigned as program director at WKQX and returned for my second of three stints at those "magic" call letters: WJMK. It was there I had the opportunity to meet and work with the legendary Dick Biondi.

My favorite promotion while I was doing the morning show on Magic 104 was in 1988. We took a group of listeners to Hollywood. It included a bus tour of movie stars' homes, a night at a comedy club and best of all a limo ride and tickets to the 60th *Academy Awards*. At that time the ceremony was held at the Shrine Auditorium.

The night of the ceremony Mary Lou and I arrived early at the auditorium, so I could get set up in the press tent. But we did get to experience walking the Red Carpet. We noticed a number of women in the viewing stands outside dressed as the Glenn Close character in *Fatal Attraction*. When we got inside, I went off to my broadcast table and Mary Lou stayed in the lobby in anticipation of seeing all the stars arrive. One of the waiters passing out drinks saw her and told her exactly where to stand to have the best view of everyone arriving. He told her to expect actor Robert Stack to be the first celebrity to arrive and he was right.

Meanwhile, the table I was assigned to was being shared by Howard Stern and his co-host Robin Quivers, who were recording their show to be broadcast the next morning in New York City. I had fun listening to some of their banter. They didn't interview any of the stars but had fun talking about them. I was the brunt of a few barbs on the air but I found out that off the air he was a nice guy.

The advantage of being in the press tent was I could now interview the Academy Award winners and presenters after they came off stage. They included Cher in her almost see-through dress, Michael Douglas and Sean Connery. While I was backstage, Mary Lou was sitting in the balcony during the show. When the broadcast was over we realized we hadn't arranged for a place to meet. She was standing there looking for me in the lobby when she heard a voice behind her say, "Keep it moving, Daahling." She turned around and it was Billy Crystal doing his Fernando voice. We eventually found each other, and our limo took us back to the hotel. We went to the bar for a nightcap and shared stories about what we did, who we saw and all the fun we had that evening.

I really enjoyed my second stint doing the morning show at Magic 104. Eventually, though, it was time for me to "keep it moving, Daahling" and set out for my next chapter.

CHAPTER 10

From Chi-Town to Beantown

"Long Train Runnin'" – Doobie Brothers
"Dirty Water" – The Standels
"Saturday in the Park" – Chicago

IN THE SUMMER OF 1989, I WAS LET GO FROM WJMK IN Chicago and was replaced by Fred Winston. I couldn't find another job in the city. Such is life in the world of radio.

In early 1990 I was working for the Chicago Bulls, but I still didn't have a job in radio. An old friend, Dave Van Dyke, called me and asked if I would fly to Boston and monitor his CBS Oldies station WODS-FM. Dave was the former program director of WODS and was eventually promoted to general manager of the station after his boss, John Gehron, resigned to join Pyramid Broadcasting and manage WNUA in Chicago. I first met Dave in New York at WOR-FM. He was the board-operator for my show!

The next time we met he was working at WDAI in Chicago as air-talent. This time he's a general manager of a CBS FM radio station!

I arrived in Boston for that monitor project and had a room waiting for me at a hotel near the radio station in the Downtown Crossing area. This was long before laptop computers, so I brought a bulky word processor with me from my home in Arlington Heights, IL. I listened to the station extensively for a day and a half and took lots of notes. I also had a Sony Walkman that I used when I would explore the streets of Boston during that time, so I wouldn't miss anything.

After a couple of days Dave invited me to dinner at a restaurant on Charles Street to talk about what observations I might have. I presented him with typed written pages of comments and recommendations. I felt the radio station sounded very good, but it could be a lot better. I really liked the air-talent, but the music focus needed to be addressed.

After dinner Dave and I went to his apartment on Beacon Hill and we spent the rest of the evening with his wife, Denise, discussing radio, films, careers and families. When it was time to leave for the hotel, Dave walked me across the Boston Common towards the hotel and said he wasn't going to let me leave Boston without committing to the Program Director position at WODS.

I was very surprised. I thought it was just one friend helping another by providing a fresh ear to the radio station. I had been out of work for several months and I told him I was interested in the position but first I needed to talk it over with Mary Lou.

When I returned home, I told Mary Lou I really wanted the job so we decided to move to Boston. Shannon was a senior in high school and Amy was in middle school. We agreed we would let them finish their school year before the three of them would move to Boston to join me. I would go to Boston by myself first. The radio station arranged for me to live in a rented condominium in an area of the city called The North End. It's home to the greatest Italian restaurants in the city. Some of our oldest American landmarks stand on narrow stone streets that resemble old European cities. Since I've always been interested in early American history, it was a treat to live in the same neighborhood as the Old North Church and Paul Revere's home.

On Saturday nights in the summertime, lots of people are out on the streets enjoying the Catholic Church festivals featuring wonderful Italian food, music and the church processions. I enjoyed stopping by these celebrations for a taste of the delicious food and I always remembered to take the cannoli.

I also had to resign from the public address announcer job at the Chicago Bulls. I had been the PA guy for about 14 seasons and the resignation was rather abrupt. The team acknowledged me before my last game and presented me with a beautiful inscribed Rado wristwatch and a Bulls jersey and I did the introductions from center court under a spotlight. When each Bulls player was introduced, he would come and shake my hand including Scottie Pippen and Michael Jordan. Television sports reporters interviewed me before the game and Mary Lou, Shannon & Amy all had VIP seats.

After a few weeks at WODS, I had times of self-doubt of whether I could do the job. There was so much responsibility put on my shoulders that involved more than just programming the radio station. I would often call Mary Lou with my concerns and she always offered support to build my self-confidence. I'm glad she did. The job provided the experience I needed for what would come next.

Once the family joined me in Boston, we purchased a condominium in Brookline. Our daughters were in school and Mary Lou had a job working in the Dean's office at Boston University. The radio station was enjoying remarkable success in ratings and revenue and Mary Lou and I were feeling more at home all the time.

Senior management in New York arranged CBS FM radio station programming meetings in Boston and asked me to arrange for evening social activities. One of those events was an evening at Fenway Park for a Boston Red Sox game. I was able to get great seats for the CBS program directors and senior management. I also made sure each person had an official Red Sox hat – the same hat the players wore. I'll never forget Joe McCoy from WCBS-FM in New York refused to wear his saying he was a die-hard Yankees fan. Even after a few beers we couldn't change his mind. Everyone had a great time and I think the Red Sox won!

Any baseball fan would appreciate watching a game in the stadium that legendary players like Babe Ruth, Ted Williams and Carl Yastrzemski all called home. Watching baseballs bounce off the Green Monster was something I never thought I'd see for myself.

When the CBS radio station in Los Angeles, KODJ, continued to struggle, CBS executives in New York decided to send Dave Van Dyke to Los Angeles to stop the downward trend. They changed the call letters from KODJ to KCBS-FM hoping it would spark new interest in the station similar to the enormous success of WCBS-FM in New York City.

Dave's replacement in Boston was Bennett Zier who worked for CBS sales in New York at the radio network level. Bennett is a very likeable guy who brought a different kind of positive atmosphere to WODS. The first thing Bennett did when he arrived in Boston was invite me to dinner. He asked me, "Did I take your job?" Since the radio station was growing and there had been precedent that the program director became general manager, I think Bennett wanted to make sure there were no hard feelings. I assured him there weren't. We became good friends. My daughter Amy was the primary baby-sitter for his children and Mary Lou and I would spend many Sundays at their home in Weston. The momentum that Dave Van Dyke and I started in 1990 was really taking hold and we became the number one station in Boston for adults 25-54 in the fall of 1991.

I've always had a soft spot for WODS. Our listeners were very passionate and loyal. We had huge crowds for our free open air Saturday evening oldies concerts at City Hall Plaza during the summer featuring artists like Lesley Gore, Jay & The Americans and Paul Revere & the Raiders. Since the concerts were free, it always drew large crowds of people of all ages and from all walks of life.

I'd hear WODS almost everywhere I'd go. Our air staff had a very unique connection with their listeners. They all had history with the city, so their names were all very familiar. Our morning man included the city in his name: Austin of Boston. Paula Street was middays with a huge following. Mike Adams, Sandy Benson, Mike Finnegan – who had a great Boston accent – and Jay Gordon filled out the air-talent lineup. Jay was the ultimate expert on everything Elvis Presley. And local legend Little Walter was on the weekends with rare audio versions of the hit songs. Walter had access to the multiple takes of recording sessions. This was the early days of music being archived in a digital format and Walter was one of the professionals that record companies trusted to convert

153

the recordings. He would feature some of these outtakes on his weekend shows. Some of them would include songs where an artist might flub a word or even forget some of the lyrics. I was so very lucky to work with these professionals.

We enjoyed living in Boston because of all it had to offer. And there is something very special about celebrating the 4th of July in Boston along the Charles River watching the fireworks overhead and listening to the Boston Pops live.

Mary Lou and I were expecting our third child and the condo we lived in was so different from what we had experienced before. We knew we needed more room. We decided it was time to buy a house. One weekend we found a home in Marlborough, Massachusetts that we loved, and we wanted to make a commitment. Monday morning I met with WODS General Manager Bennett Zier and I was excited to tell him about the house we found. He asked if we had made an offer and I said, "Not yet. We're planning on going back out this next weekend." He replied, "Nope. Go back to your office and call New York." I wasn't expecting that reply. He wanted me to speak to Rod Calarco who was in charge of the FM Division at CBS Headquarters.

I first met Rod when I joined WODS. He would visit Boston often on business and luckily was able to join us for one of our Saturday night outdoor free concerts. After the show he joined some of the staff for dinner. This is where Mary Lou and Rod got to know each other. He convinced her to share some steamers and longnecks. She didn't know what that meant but agreed. Once the mussels and a bucket of beers arrived, she told the waiter she probably needed another bucket just for herself. This has been a joke between the three of us, and our friendship has lasted to this day.

After I left Bennett's office, I called Rod and he asked me to fly to New York that next morning for a meeting. It was then I learned I was being transferred to Los Angeles to program KCBS-FM. The radio station was a 60's and early 70's-based oldies station with the majority of their music post 1964 and pre 1972.

In the meeting, Rod told me I was to try to fix the existing oldies format at KCBS-FM to improve their ratings and if that didn't work, "Throw in some grenades and start over."

CHAPTER 11

From Beantown to Tinseltown

"Soul Man" – Sam & Dave
"Green Onions" – Booker T and the MG's
"Good Vibrations" – The Beach Boys

Now it was time to head west to a radio job that presented the biggest challenges of my career. It was also the opportunity of a lifetime. My bosses in New York told me I would get access to whatever it took to turn the station into a winner. And they lived up to that promise. I couldn't wait to get started.

The announcement of the move would be delayed until early 1992. Mary Lou and I secretly flew to LA between Christmas and New Year's to look for a place to live but we didn't find anything we liked on that trip. We only told our daughters of what was happening and had them keep it secret.

Once the announcement was made, I said goodbye to the great staff of WODS and flew to Los Angeles again. I lived in a beautiful hotel in the heart of Beverly Hills for the first few weeks. I found it to be quiet and peaceful – except for a few days in late January.

There was a song being played on all the contemporary hit radio stations in early 1992 called *Gonna Make You Sweat (Everybody Dance Now)* by C + C Music Factory. That song drove me crazy. I didn't like it at all, and my kids teased me about it whenever they could. One day I walked out of my room at the hotel and found that members of C + C Music Factory had rooms across the hall from mine. They were in town from New York. That was OK but on the evening of January 27th, the group won 5 *American Music Awards* at the Shrine Auditorium in LA. Where do you think they partied all night? Right! It was across the hall from my room! It was a Monday night and after a long day at work, I needed to get some sleep. I realized that wasn't going to happen. Maybe I should have gone over and knocked on the door and tried to join the fun. When I told my kids about it, they laughed and never let me forget it.

I was able to find a home for the family in about 10 days. Two months after the family moved west, our son Tommy was born.

KCBS-FM, KNX-AM and KCBS-TV were all located in the historic Columbia Square facility on Sunset Boulevard in Hollywood. I drove on the lot my first day and was pleasantly surprised to find a primo parking space with my name on it! This building had so much history associated with it. At one time it housed the Columbia Records recording studio where artists like Janis Joplin, Bob Dylan, Barbra Streisand, The Beach Boys and so many others recorded their albums. George Nicholaw was the senior CBS executive at Columbia Square. On my first day, he took me on a tour to see where the pilot for the *I Love Lucy* TV show had been filmed. The stage and curtain were still there but the multi-level audience space in the studio had been turned into lots of storage cages.

KCBS-FM featured legendary jocks like Charlie Tuna, "Machine Gun" Kelly, and "The Real" Don Steele. These were the guys I admired and listened to on air-checks in the early days of my career when they were on "Boss Radio 93 KHJ." They were the gold standard of rock jocks.

My first priority at KCBS-FM was reviewing the station's music playlist. I compared that to K-Earth 101 radio who had been in the same oldies format for over 20 years. KRTH are the official call letters and they were dominant in the ratings. However, the two radio stations were playing basically the same songs.

I had to differentiate the music. K-Earth was playing lots of Motown but very little by artists like The Isley Brothers, Sam & Dave, Booker T. & The MGs and Aretha Franklin. I added a number of those artists in rotation and we witnessed an immediate bump in listeners and time spent listening for KCBS-FM. It was an improvement, but we still had a long way to go.

I also focused on K-Earth's tight playlist with some short on-air promotion announcements. In radio lingo they're called sweepers. One of them was "We don't play the same hundred oldies over and over. We play *all* the good songs on Oldies 93." That caused an immediate reaction. I heard from friends who had connections with K-Earth that they noticed in their call out research the sweepers were very effective. Soon they launched sweepers of their own saying they've added hundreds and hundreds of great songs to their playlist. Then I began hearing some of the artists we had added. I countered with a sweeper that said "Oldies 93 plays the best oldies on the radio." K-Earth's consultant, Bill Drake reportedly said he loved that sweeper and decided to steal it. He immediately called the station's jingle producer, Johnny Mann, and requested a jingle within 24 hours singing: "The best oldies on the radio, K-Earth 101."

A legendary Los Angeles radio personality contacted me a few weeks after I made some changes. Robert W. Morgan was doing mornings at KMPC-AM. Robert was at one time the king of morning radio at KHJ. He found my email address and asked if we could arrange a telephone conversation. I responded by giving him my cell phone number and suggesting we talk the following Saturday afternoon. He called while I was looking after my son who was napping at the time. We had a great conversation that lasted over an hour. He said he enjoyed the changes I was making and shared some stories about the old days at KHJ.

My first major station concert was shortly after I arrived. Oldies 93 produced a Rock n Roll Oldies Show at The Forum in late 1992. I wanted to get some legendary performers to headline the show. There were two in particular: Jerry Lee Lewis and Fats Domino. It wasn't a problem getting Jerry Lee to perform as long as we hired his manager to accompany Lewis at all times. I'm not sure why that was needed but I can tell you Lewis forgot the words to "Whole Lotta Shakin' Goin' On" in the middle of the song. The audience helped him out by singing it for him. I couldn't get Fats Domino to sign-on for the show because his manager said Fats was worried that he couldn't get a good meal in Los Angeles. That's why he wanted to stay in New Orleans. Huh?

This back and forth battle was fun. In analyzing the ratings situation I was facing, K-Earth had a cumulative audience several times larger than KCBS-FM so it pretty much neutralized all of our sweepers. Before we were to make any major changes, there were a few things to try. I didn't know then I'd have to go through a riot first.

In April of '92, several white Los Angeles Police Officers were acquitted of using excessive force on a black man named Rodney King during a traffic stop. A video had been taken of the beating of King and was shown on television. Once the verdict was announced, riots broke out all over Los Angeles. Fires were set, stores were looted, innocent people were beaten and there was rage in the streets. I could see huge plumes of black smoke covering the city from my office in Hollywood. It was a very tense and ugly time in LA. The next day Dave Van Dyke and I called all non-essential employees at home and said they did not have to report to work. Everything stopped due to the civil unrest. The radio station continued to broadcast but on a subdued posture. The CBS television and radio studios at Columbia Square were all secure.

It didn't take long for things at the radio station to get back to normal. I received a call from another legendary radio talent in LA. This time he was looking for a job. It was "Humble" Harve Miller. He was one of the KHJ "Boss Jocks" and was a real character. Now he was doing the nighttime show on K-Earth. We met at the famous Jerry's Deli in Studio City. We worked out the deal and he was our new nighttime talent. Rick Sietsema was the engineering supervisor at the time. When I announced that I had hired Harve in a department head meeting, Rick's head dropped and hit the conference room table. We all looked at him and when he straightened up, he said, "Tell Harve he cannot and must not tinker with any of the equipment." Apparently, he had a reputation of claiming he was a Mr. Fixit when he felt something wasn't working correctly. That actually happened one night when Harve called me at home and said he thought one of the CD players wasn't operating right, so he offered to take it apart while he was on the air and fix it. I told him absolutely not and he should put a piece of tape over the machine and I'd have the engineers look at it the next morning.

There was another voice of concern about me hiring "Humble" Harve. It came from the President of CBS Radio, Nancy Widmann. Harve had served a stretch in prison for manslaughter in the 1971 death of his wife, Mary. Dave Van Dyke and I heard a story about this event from Harve's longtime friend and co-worker "The Real" Don Steele. I cannot confirm the accuracy of the story because I've heard other details, so I won't repeat it. I assured Nancy that Harve had served his time in prison and it had been almost 20 years since his release. He had since worked for a number of radio stations and even did voice work for a movie. He sounded great on K-Earth. I knew having Harve on Oldies 93 would help us and hurt K-Earth.

Back to the battle of the two oldies radio stations. It was our turn to do something different. We created a major television campaign with Frankie Avalon and Annette Funicello as spokespersons. We shot the TV commercial in Annette's living room in Encino, California and it provided me with the opportunity to meet a lady that I grew up admiring as a teen. She was the star of the *Mickey Mouse Club* on television and every young guy fell in love with her. She was also the star of many beach themed movies that had the word *bikini* in its title. Her co-star in these films was Frankie. Now here I was sitting on her couch between takes and talking to her about her career. She had been diagnosed with multiple sclerosis five years earlier. She kept it secret until 1992.

She was kind and gracious and along with Frankie, made a terrific television commercial for Oldies 93. We launched the commercial and of course, K-Earth had a response.

They announced an enormous contest. The station was going to give away $1,000 every hour! Every Hour…Every Day! And they did. It was a very effective contest/promotion and it was obvious we had to do something radically different.

At that time K-Earth was owned by Beasley Broadcasting. The fellow who was in charge of the company and the station was an old friend of mine: Simon T. Simon and I worked together at WLS and we even lived in the same apartment building in downtown Chicago. His place was the gathering point for The Clique to watch *Saturday Night Live* during its first season. Simon pulled out all the stops and KCBS-FM couldn't recover.

It took us a while to realize the oldies format belonged exclusively to K-Earth. Executives at CBS in New York confirmed their original directive to me to explore a new format. As a matter of fact, we knew for sure we needed to change when we hosted an oldies concert at the fairgrounds in Costa Mesa, California. We gave away lots of tickets and heavily promoted the show for weeks. On stage the night of the concert in front of a huge Oldies 93 banner, Martha Reeves of Martha and the Vandellas said, "Thank you so much for coming tonight and a special thanks to K-Earth for inviting us to perform." That slammed the door shut on the oldies format.

CHAPTER 12

The Arrow

"Night Moves" – Bob Seger
"Heartache Tonight" – The Eagles
"Hit Me with Your Best Shot" – Pat Benatar

W E KNEW WE HAD TO DO SOMETHING DIFFERENT.
We had to come up with a format that wouldn't be confused with
K-Earth or any other Los Angeles radio station.

We hired The Research Group to conduct a format search
project in Los Angeles. This company was highly regarded to
provide options and it involved extensive telephone research plus
focus groups of targeted demographics. It took a few months to
get results. It was worth it. We found the following to be the ideal
format: something similar to oldies that focuses on newer music
of the 70's and 80's. In addition, the on-air talent would play more
of a background role.

The names that were most attractive to our target audience were: "All Rock and Roll Everything", "All Rock and Roll Oldies" and "All Rock and Roll 70's & 80's." The strongest of the three was "All Rock and Roll Oldies" so we began plotting how we would use the name on the air. We started by writing: "A R R O" as an acronym on a white board. We thought of names like The Eagle, The Quake and a few others. Then one of us walked up to the board and added a W to the end. "ARROW" was on the white board and we loved it. It was aggressive. It was in motion. It was different and it even provided us with an audio signature. The sound of an arrow leaving a bow and striking a target is what we needed to create. I called a sound artist engineer in Boston we had used for a television commercial and described what I wanted. I used my voice to try to create what I was thinking. He worked on it and just days after we launched the new format, we had the perfect audio sound effect. We used the sound between two songs on occasion without talk.

One of the unfortunate side issues with creating a whole new format was I had to say goodbye to the legendary talent. That was very difficult for me. But being the professionals they were, they understood it was just business.

Before I parted ways with my current on-air staff, I had to secretly build a new jock lineup for this new format. I put a blind ad in a trade newspaper and had all the correspondence and air-checks sent to the newspaper's address. The trade paper forwarded the material to my home address and I listened to everything that was submitted. I found two jocks, Dave White and Kevin Machado, who I thought would sound great in this new format, so I called them. I told them I was a program director of a major market station and I liked their work. I asked if they were willing and capable to relocate on a moment's notice. They eagerly said yes. I then revealed who I was and where I was calling from and said I wanted them to keep it secret. They promised they would. A couple of weeks before the launch date, I called them again and said I was sending airline tickets, information where they would be living temporarily and other instructions. I told them to be ready to move to Los Angeles. I reminded them it is still secret. When they came into town, Mary Lou picked them up at the airport and took them to their short-term corporate housing. They didn't know the new format or what air-shift they would work. The only thing they knew was they had to be at the radio station's conference room at 2 p.m. on the launch date, September 10, 1993.

Since our music was going to be far different from the 50's, 60's and early 70's oldies, I had to restock our music library. I couldn't ask record companies for help because I needed to keep the description of our new format super-secret, so I went out and bought a new music library. I'd spend anywhere from $400 to $600 at area record stores and when questioned at checkout I'd say it was my birthday and this is a present to me from me. We were still playing CDs at this time. I also built the new format in the RCS Music Scheduling System and catalogued CD numbers and track numbers. Mary Lou typed and sealed the identifying numbers on the CD casings and I would transport them to the radio station over a couple of weeks and lock them in the cabinet in my office. This was so secret that this preliminary work on the music couldn't be done in my office. The new format was created on my dining room table.

I asked one of the late evening jocks to meet me at the station one afternoon and suggested we walk around the block. I told Gary

Moore on that walk I wanted him to be the morning man of a new format and told him to keep it secret and prepare to move to that shift on the launch date.

Dave Van Dyke and I were approving artwork on new logos and a new television commercial and everything was coming together. We leaked the launch date and the new format was kept a total secret until the moment we put it on the air.

Arrow 93 was born at 3pm on September 10, 1993 with the first song being "Old Time Rock and Roll" by Bob Seger followed by "Purple Haze" by Jimi Hendrix.

One of the first people that contacted me once we launched Arrow 93 was Harry Nilsson's agent. Harry was a Grammy Award winning singer/songwriter. He is best known for his song "Everybody's Talkin'." Harry lived in suburban Agoura Hills, California. His agent told me Harry loved the station so much he would drive around all day listening to it. The agent said Harry had a gift for me and had left it with the security guard on the first floor of Columbia Square. I went down to the security desk and found a digital audio tape. I took it upstairs and asked the production director to play it for me. I was surprised to hear that Harry had taken the master tape of his song "Me & My Arrow" and re-sang one part: "Me & My Arrow – 93 and Me." I used that track as a sweeper for years. It was a wonderful gift. I was deeply saddened to learn of Harry's death in January, 1994 and I regret I never had the chance to thank him in person.

Other celebrities were fans of The Arrow as well. Charlie Sheen and David Lee Roth called to inquire about having a role with the station. I wrote some liners for both of them to record and I used them in sweepers. They both have distinctive voices our listeners could easily recognize. Our night-time jocks got telephone calls requesting songs from Jay Leno and the writers of *The Tonight Show* who would be listening to Arrow 93 while they were working.

My family was invited to a NASCAR Race at California Speedway. We found ourselves sitting with Journey's Steve Perry. Steve and I were sitting next to each other and he asked me a question about one of the drivers that I couldn't answer. My 7-year-old son spoke up and answered Steve's question and surprised both of us with his knowledge of NASCAR drivers. Steve then asked me to move and asked Tommy to sit next to him so they could talk about the race.

Several months later I developed a "Mystery Voice" contest on The Arrow and invited Steve Perry to the studio to record his voice. We then had a chance to catch up and we talked about Pismo Beach, California being one of our favorite places to visit.

Our station was one of the very first in Los Angeles to have a presence on the internet. We had one of the first websites! It was so new that we were not able to use numbers in its address. It was simply: arrowfm.com. We had photos of the jocks, stories about contests and promotions and whatever else we could think of. This was before we could stream the audio of the radio station.

I was fortunate to have a terrific staff to back me up. Music Directors Billy Sabatini and Clark Macy were invaluable to our success and my assistant Sally Bowman kept the administrative duties of payroll and scheduling letter-perfect. Billy and an intern, Tim Suing, educated themselves on how to operate the website which was critically important. We were able to bring all of that in-house from the beginning.

Eventually Sabatini left The Arrow and was one of the early pioneers in satellite radio. He became Vice President of World Space, Inc. serving huge populations in Asia and Africa. He then went on to be General Manager of Radio Sawa Network providing terrestrial radio networks in the Middle East and North Africa.

Tim Suing went on to be a successful attorney. And Macy became a health care administration official.

I was also lucky to be able to work with some other well-known Los Angeles jocks which helped in making Arrow 93 a little more familiar to LA radio listeners. Among them were Bob Coburn, Mary Price and Joe Benson.

Bob Coburn was known nationwide as the host of the syndicated show *Rockline*. Bob would interview rock stars from every era. He was an expert on not only classic rock but contemporary rock which lent his appeal to multiple formats.

Bob invited me to attend some of his interviews at a studio on Sepulveda Boulevard and one caught my eye and ear. His interview with Ray Manzarek of The Doors was fascinating not only for what they talked about but what Manzarek was doing with his hands the whole time. His fingers were on the desk and it appeared he was playing an imaginary keyboard. Months later I arranged to have Ray come to the Arrow 93 studios to be interviewed live by Joe Benson and I asked an intern to get a full-length portable keyboard. The engineering department hooked it up to the audio chain and when Joe asked a question about a particular Doors' song, Manzarek would play it in the background of the interview. The same thing would happen when Joe asked about Jim Morrison. Manzarek would play an identifiable Doors melody in the background. I think it really added to the entertainment value.

Arrow 93 was continuing to build an audience. The classic rock station in LA, KLSX, dropped their music format and went all talk. K-Earth was still successful, but Arrow 93 had built a significant audience of former K-Earth and KLSX listeners. The station was making nice profits which made our New York bosses very happy.

Many other radio stations around the country wanted to launch their versions of the Arrow Format. When their programmers called to ask for advice, I cautioned them that the Los Angeles version of this format was specifically built for Southern California. I told them they needed to take the basic elements of the format and build on that for their individual market. The ones who did were successful and I'm very proud of that.

We had become very comfortable in LA. One daughter was in college, our other daughter was in high school and our son was less than two years old. However, we didn't anticipate what was next.

On the morning of January 17th, 1994 at 4:30 a.m. we were awakened by a 6.7 magnitude earthquake. Mary Lou and I jumped out of bed just before a TV that was on top of my armoire came crashing down on our bed. We raced to get the kids and we went downstairs. The power was out everywhere and I had to manually raise the garage door which was no easy task. I backed our SUV out to the driveway, and we spent hours sitting in the car. Since all the lights were out everywhere, you could see millions of stars in the sky. That was a very rare sight for LA.

Coincidentally just days before this happened, I had a staff meeting at the radio station and we revised our earthquake protocols. As a result, everyone knew what needed to be done. We started simulcasting with KNX-AM for the rest of the day. I was given a two-way radio to keep at home in the event of an emergency just like this so I walked to the top of a hill overlooking the San Fernando Valley and did a live report for KNX on what I could see. I learned later from Mary Lou's mother that the CBS Radio Network featured my report in a nationwide newscast. A few fires had broken out. Cars were still on the freeway but they were moving slowly. It was a very strange experience!

This scared the hell out of us – both at home and at the radio station. CBS Radio had counselors come into the facility and I, along with several other staff members, attended those sessions. Meanwhile at home, Mary Lou and I looked closely at everything hanging over our kids' beds and we stocked up on new flashlights, batteries and jugs of water. There was major destruction to some freeways and bridges but Angelinos are very resilient and life got back to normal despite many aftershocks. We are very thankful that no one in the family was injured and there was only minor damage to the house we were living in.

A few days after the quake and during the aftershock episodes, I added the song "I Love L.A." by Randy Newman to the playlist and it generated a story in the *Los Angeles Times*. A reporter asked me about it and I said that despite the danger of earthquakes, California is a wonderful place to live and the telephone reaction from listeners was all very positive.

Fortunately, the radio station didn't suffer any damage in the quake. Things got back to normal.

Arrow 93 had some terrific television commercials during this time. We also played with some new technology to try to attract listeners while they were in their car. Dave Van Dyke and I arranged to have the ability to send an electronic signal to several billboards situated on busy freeways that provided a message in lights of the name of the artist of the song we were playing at that moment. Some of this technology sounds so elementary now but at the time it was rather mind-blowing. As a matter of fact, we spoke on the telephone to the man who developed the billboard message technology and asked if it could be used on the internet for a "now playing" function. He didn't answer. After we hung-up we had a feeling that technology was already in the works.

The success of Arrow 93 created a buzz in the industry both at home and abroad. The National Association of Broadcasters contacted me and asked if I'd speak to a group of European broadcasters in Amsterdam about the research process and how important it was to a successful format change. I jumped at the chance and made arrangements to fly with Mary Lou and our young son Tommy to spend several days in Holland. At the event I met and made friends with several European broadcasters. I became reacquainted with a few British radio programmers that I had met at an NAB Convention in Boston while I was working there. At that time, they invited me to their facility near Cambridge where I had the opportunity to speak to their staff about what was happening on the radio back home in the U.S. And I kept in contact with Dutch radio executives I had met in Amsterdam for several years.

We really enjoyed our time in Amsterdam. Even though it was in November, the weather didn't stop us from walking and exploring the city. We even had a free day where we took a train to Brussels. Then we flew back home to warmer weather and we headed to the beach.

There were many days Mary Lou, Tommy and I would take a weekday off and spend it on Zuma Beach in Malibu. I called them *monitor days* meaning I'd spend the day listening to the radio station without the meetings and phone calls. But in reality, it was a time of wonderful therapy to sit in the sun and stare out at the Pacific. All the tension and stress of long hours and tough decisions would disappear, and serenity would take hold. It was a wonderful way to recharge my interest in working hard.

However, it wasn't all work and no play. There were many concerts featuring the superstars of rock. Rod Stewart at the Hollywood Bowl. The Rolling Stones with the Red Hot Chili Peppers at the Rose Bowl. Paul McCartney at the Staples Center and a private sound-check with Arrow 93 listeners. We were involved with the reunion of The Eagles in their "Hell Freezes Over" tour at the Staples Center. And the night of the U2 concert at Staples was a show we'll always remember.

We were also blessed by living in a great neighborhood. We lived on a cul-de-sac with many families who also had young children. On warm evenings we'd all be outside. The kids and the dads would play softball in the street. The families would vacation together around Labor Day. We'd all meet in Scottsdale, AZ at a resort. We'd go from hot weather to hotter weather.

We were also fortunate to reconnect with an old friend, Paul Clarke. I mentioned earlier he was with us on our first date when we all worked together at WEAM radio and was a groomsman in our wedding. Paul was now a political consultant. He was married to the former U.S. Congresswoman Bobbi Fiedler. They were a terrific resource for us as newcomers to Southern California. We were so happy to renew our friendship.

New Year's Eve, 1999 was spent at the radio station. Senior management required us to be there as a precaution because of concerns about Y2K. A few staff members joined us to deal with whatever might happen IF all the computers crashed. Fortunately, it was a non-event. Mary Lou and Tommy joined me in my office, and we all wound up on the fire escape watching fireworks all around the Hollywood area.

During this era various consultants inside and outside the company worked on convincing us that we needed to build a stronger morning show. Their idea centered around replacing our music-oriented show with an ensemble consisting of a group of voices talking about whatever they had on their minds. In other words, less music and lots of talk. I didn't care for the idea because of the statistics we learned in our extensive market research. But the pressure was building. We eventually brought in a show from another part of the country and it didn't take long for me to realize it was a mistake. This show spent more time talking about their smaller market and when I attempted to take control of producing the show, I was shot down. The reaction from our listeners was overwhelming. They disliked the show. I knew it wasn't working and I told senior management something had to change. Before I could do anything, the group packed up and left town on their own in the middle of the week without telling us. I looked at this experience as a lesson to trust my instincts.

Once I learned the group had left without notice, I contacted Joe Benson, who had moved to the afternoon shift, and asked him to be on the air the next morning – back in his old shift. He and the rest of the morning crew were there the next day and the complaint calls stopped. The mood around the radio station improved drastically.

I usually went for long walks early in the morning before I showered and drove to work. One morning I was all set to go and for some reason I turned on the television in the family room and saw early coverage of the September 11th attack on the World Trade Center in New York. The first news accounts were about a plane crashing into one of the towers and as the coverage expanded, I decided to stay and watch what was happening. Mary Lou and I, like everyone else, were horrified by what we witnessed. By the time I showered and was driving to the radio station, more information was being released and the magnitude of the attacks became more frightening. I called the hotline and instructed Joe Benson to dump all commercials and songs and carry KNX-AM live. We continued to simulcast the all-news station for several hours.

It is impossible to summarize how this attack affected everyone. We realized there would be a strong feeling of patriotism growing around the country. That became evident at a concert that we had already scheduled at the Queen Mary Park in Long Beach. Among the acts that we had booked was Jefferson Airplane including lead singer Grace Slick. This was her first appearance with the band in a long time. When the group came out on stage, Grace led the crowd with a "USA USA" chant.

In 2002 CBS Radio held a manager's meeting in New York. One evening I skipped a social event and took a subway downtown to see Ground Zero. I walked several blocks from the subway station and passed endless memorials to the thousands of people killed in the attack. There were photos of loved ones with candles, letters and cards addressed to the people who had died. Eventually I found a temporary platform that was built overlooking the recovery effort. It was a very emotional night.

During the years I was at KCBS-FM, the company went through various ownership changes. Westinghouse bought CBS and kept the

CBS name. CBS bought Infinity Broadcasting and Viacom bought CBS. Once all of this happened, CBS now owned a number of radio stations in LA including stations that we had been competing against. Arrow 93 had already knocked KLSX out of the classic rock format. Now the all talk KLSX and oldies K-Earth were CBS owned stations. Dave Van Dyke was let go and the manager of KLSX was now the manager of both KLSX and Arrow 93.

I was asked to make yet another on-air talent change. The talent involved was someone I admired. However, I had learned the lesson of not trusting my gut a year earlier. Therefore, I recommended against the hiring saying it would be a big mistake.

As I mentioned, consolidation was happing everywhere and as a result I had to leave Arrow 93. The new managers decided to go ahead and make changes to the music and air talent. It didn't work.

One of the managers who decided on making those changes eventually called me a year later to tell me that I was right all along.

Business is business and I understand nothing lasts forever. I do believe that the decade I spent building and programming Arrow 93 was the one of the best experiences of my life. I am very proud of what we accomplished.

My next job was as a consultant to a radio group in New Mexico. My office was in Albuquerque which was a mere 60 miles away from "Sacred Lujack Mountain." I looked forward to spending some time with my "Charming and Delightful" old friend.

CHAPTER 13

You Should Be Nicer to Larry

"I Can't Help Myself (Sugar Pie Honey Bunch)" – Four Tops
"Lightnin' Strikes" – Lou Christie
"Baby Now That I Found You" – The Foundations

IN 2003 I WAS ASKED TO RETURN TO CHICAGO AND build another radio station. I had only been in Albuquerque for a few months. I resigned from my position and headed back to Chicago. Mary Lou and Tommy were still living in our home in Los Angeles. It was a difficult move having to leave our home, our daughters and our first grandchild.

John Gehron was Market Manager for the Clear Channel radio stations in Chicago. The company moved a radio frequency from Southern Illinois to Berwyn to broadcast on 1690 kHz. This frequency was relatively new because the FCC had recently expanded the AM dial and not every car radio could receive that

179

signal. Nonetheless I came up with WRLL as the call letters. The RLL was to stand for Real Oldies and the format would be music from the 50's and 60's. It was a little different than the other radio stations in town. The morning show was live and the rest of the day was voice-tracked. I hired former Chicago talent who were living in the city and various parts of the country. Ron Smith was our Music Director and Len O'Kelly was our Production Director. Both guys did daily shows. Kathy Worthington was our newsperson and a key part of the morning show. The four of us were the only full-time employees of the radio station.

I wanted Ron Smith as our Music Director because there wasn't anyone in Chicago who knew more about oldies music than Ron. He had published a number of books with charts and feature material about the songs and the artists. The 24-hour scheduling of music was all managed by him. Ron also had a daily show which he voice-tracked, where he shared his knowledge of the music and the artists.

Len O'Kelly handled all of the production of the station and did all the voice-tracks for the overnight show. The rest of the air talent would load their voice-tracks from their home studios and Len would quality control all of them.

I had known Kathy for a long time. She was a former WGN radio reporter and also worked at WLS. She is the mother of broadcasters Rafer Weigel and Jennifer Weigel.

I asked Larry Lujack if he'd like to do the morning show with me. I told him with this new technology, he could do his part from his home in Santa Fe, New Mexico. He agreed and we set it up. We had worked together for so long and were very familiar with each other's style and delivery. It was very easy to make it sound as though he was sitting right next to me in the Chicago studio.

I arrived at the radio station before 4 a.m. each weekday morning for show prep and I would print emails and make photocopies of newspaper stories and entertainment magazine articles. I would fax all these pages to Larry in Santa Fe. Larry particularly enjoyed the emails from listeners. He had fun with the emails criticizing the signal or complaining about something he had said over the air. Of the estimated 50 pages I would fax to him daily, he'd usually use only a handful of them.

The fax function that was built into his answering machine was about the only high technology Larry could handle. He used to say that he was part of the Hi-Tech Backlash. I'd check in with him to confirm that he had received everything and on several occasions he would ask me to fax the material again because he ran out of paper! Once I confirmed he received everything, I would go into the secure master control facility and push the necessary buttons to establish the audio link with the equipment in Larry's house. He would either tell me he could hear me or I could hear him in the background ruffling through papers. To be able to hear me talk, he would have to have headphones on.

The radio equipment was set up in his home office. I had the chance to see this space when I was working in Albuquerque and spent some time on the weekends with Larry in his home. Larry and Jude had their home built on top of a hill that Larry referred to as Sacred Lujack Mountain. It had a long gravel driveway to the top. His house was built in the historic adobe architectural style. It had a flat roof with containers under downspouts to capture rain water. He had large thick window blind panels he installed daily that would shield the interior from the hot New Mexico sun. The kitchen and living room areas were spacious and tastefully accented in southwestern décor. His office was another story. It was a mess. Jude told me she never went in there. There were old newspapers, yellow tablets with hand-written notes, half-eaten bagels and an overflowing trash can. It was so unlike the rest of the house.

Larry said he loved living in Santa Fe. He told me he spent hours sitting outside on a patio contemplating the world. The only thing he didn't like was the perpetual drought. As a result, some of his trees were dying or dead. He also complained about the teenagers that would party in a nearby wooded area at night. He was worried about them causing a fire.

Each morning I had to remember to tell him what the weather was in Chicago so he could ad-lib around it. One morning Larry mentioned that the foggy weather was affecting planes coming in and out of Meigs Field. He said he could see them from our high rise studio. I responded, "Uh, Lar? That's amazing you can see all that because Mayor Daley had the airport and runways demolished several months ago." His response after a long pause: "Whoops."

We had a few in-studio interviews with celebrities during this time. Earvin "Magic" Johnson stopped by once after appearing on some of the other Clear Channel stations in the Illinois Center Building. Lar' and I had fun talking hoop with him. And I appreciated "Magic" signing an autograph for my son. We interviewed dancers from the Radio City Music Hall Rockettes in the studio one morning to promote their Christmas Show at Rosemont Theatre. Before the live interview and during a song I told the women my partner is in Santa Fe and can hear everything but can't see us and I would eventually ask him if he had any questions. I didn't want them to be surprised when they heard his voice. After I had asked them about their appearance in Chicago I said "I'm sure Larry has a question or two." He said, "Right you are. I do have an important question: How many times do you have to shave your legs?" I jumped in and told them, "Ah You don't have to answer that." Their eyes were wide open and obviously they were taken by surprise with the question and the interview was over.

Larry always looked for something funny to talk about on the air. He loved it when he could play the victim. Mary Lou understood his humor and was always a good sport about it. One day he called me at home and Mary Lou answered the phone with, "He's not here." Larry responded, "Ah Mary Lou, no hi Lar? No how are you Lar? Just He's not here?" Mary Lou responded, "Oh Lar who are you kidding? You didn't call to talk to me." Naturally he turned that into a "bit" the next morning on the air. He said, "I called Little Tommy at home yesterday and of course his wife, Mary Lou has that fancy caller ID and knew it was me." Then he repeated the beginning of their conversation and started complaining that Mary Lou was rude on the phone. He was having fun with the story. Everyone in the studio was laughing. We all had fun with it. A couple of weeks later I was on a personal appearance and Mary Lou was with me. Two women came up to her and said, "You really should be nicer to Larry." They were serious. Mary Lou couldn't help but laugh. She told them, "We always give each other a hard time."

We did *Animal Stories* live every morning. We also did the *Cheap Trashy Showbiz Report* along with the *Larry Lujack Address to the Nation*. One morning in November in an episode of the *Cheap Trashy Show-Biz Report*, we wished actress/singer Connie Stevens a Happy Birthday. That same evening I ran into Connie at a Bulls game and wished her a happy birthday in person. She looked pissed and said, "It's not my fucking birthday." I told Lar about it the next day and it wasn't long until he reported hearing a story about Connie cutting in on a long line waiting to get into a ladies room during a concert. When some women complained, Connie allegedly said, "Don't you know who I am? I'm Connie Fucking Stevens." We laughed about that for a long time. And ever since then, whenever we mentioned her name, we always included her colorful *middle* name. On the air the expletive was changed to "friggin."

One of the legendary talents working for me abruptly resigned when I asked him to trim the number of ad-libs because we had lost a sizable amount of revenue over a period of a week on his show. I was told he complained to someone, "You don't tell Picasso how to paint." I had to laugh when I heard that.

The automated broadcast system that we were using reset at the top of each hour. That meant that everything that wasn't broadcast in the previous hour would be dropped and a new hour of music and commercials would be scheduled to play. This caused problems on occasion because if there was too much talk and the system reset before all of the scheduled commercials were broadcast, the commercials were then cancelled, and the radio station lost money. We needed every commercial logged to run so I had to remind the air talent that they could tell stories and have fun but be mindful that I was going to catch a lot of heat from senior management if any commercial didn't run. And if the station was going to be successful and survive, especially with a weak signal, we needed to run everything that was sold. Otherwise, everyone – even Picasso – wouldn't get paid.

Larry and I had many laughs working at Real Oldies 1690, but we knew it couldn't last. Larry used to say over the air that we'd soon go belly up. Several communities in Chicagoland couldn't hear us. We were broadcasting at a very high frequency and extremely low assigned power. Cars built before the late 1990's had AM radios that didn't go beyond 1605 kHz. In 2003 there were many cars from the 90's still on the road that had AM radios unable to tune to 1690 kHz. We would also hear from fans who lived a good distance away from Berwyn who would spot Clear Channel billboards advertising the radio station. But due to the weak signal, there was poor reception even in late model cars.

However, there were many people who *could* hear us, and they responded with great enthusiasm to the promotions we produced. These events were record-hop type dances at the Willowbrook Ballroom along Archer Avenue in Willow Springs. The turnout for every event was huge. John Gehron asked me to schedule more of them because of the revenue they brought in. At one of our first dances, Larry recorded some announcements as if he was out in the parking lot directing traffic and interrupting couples who were having fun in their car. I played the announcements from the stage and they were a big hit.

I've talked to a number of people who listened regularly, and they were saddened when we lost the opportunity to be on the air. One friend is former *Chicago Tribune* sports writer and Naismith Memorial Basketball Hall of Fame honoree Sam Smith. Sam is a huge oldies fan and is very knowledgeable about the artists and songs.

Another fan of the 50's and 60's oldies we played on Real Oldies 1690 was Patrick McCaskey, an executive of the Chicago Bears. Patrick and I became friends when our sons played basketball together in middle school. Quite often we started singing an oldie during the game much to the embarrassment of our wives. However, the rest of the team parents had fun with it.

John Gehron left the company in 2005 and we all got nervous about the future of the radio station. In 2006 I got a call at home one afternoon from a new boss informing me that Clear Channel gave or leased the frequency to another radio company, and we were all out of jobs effective immediately. I had to call everyone around the country and tell them the bad news. I was able to contact all the talent except our morning newsperson, Kathy Worthington. I left messages for her to call me but she never got them and she showed up for work early the next day. That's when she found out. When I called Larry with the news he said it didn't surprise him.

A few weeks after I left Real Oldies, two old friends helped me open the next chapter in my career. One was from another radio station in Chicago and the other was an executive of the Chicago Bulls.

But first, I want to take a moment to tell you some things that you might not know about Uncle Lar'.

CHAPTER 14

Another Side of Lujack

"Burning Love" – Elvis Presley
"Lady" – Styx
"Hard Day's Night"- The Beatles

I MET LARRY LUJACK ON MY SECOND DAY AT WLS IN June of 1972. At first, our relationship was distant because he was working out the last few days of his contract with the station having already agreed to move to WLS's chief competitor, WCFL. Once he was on CFL, I would listen to his afternoon show and enjoy his "Clunk Letter of the Day" feature. I remember hearing him while on vacation in the 60s in the Seattle/Tacoma area on KJR radio. Air talent on that station was using just their last names and Lujack was one of them.

After Larry left WLS in 1972, he and I had no contact at all except for the two brief meetings with his agent. Then one day in

1974, I received a phone call from Larry I'll never forget. A recent article in a trade publication mentioned some of the creative programming WLS was running including the *What's Your Favorite Radio Station* contest, *MusicPeople* and *Touch Tone* contests and the publication didn't attribute the creation of any of this to me. Larry called and said that the magazine didn't mention my name anywhere, but he and everyone else in the Chicago radio market knew who created those features and he wanted me to know that. That phone call meant so much to me at that time. Behind all the ego of his gruff on-air persona, there was a decent guy who didn't have to bother calling me about that, but HE DID.

During our time together as jocks at WLS, we became real close friends. Some people might call Larry "cheap." Actually, he was a little eccentric but very frugal. He always seemed to come up with very creative ways to save money. One time he called me on a Saturday morning to say he read that a denim store was selling Levi's jeans for about $10 each and he wanted us to go buy a dozen or so. I asked him if he thought his waistline might change over the next few years because what we bought now might not fit in the next year or two. He said, "Nah, I'm not putting on any weight." I laughed and said I'd pass on buying any jeans today. I'm pretty sure he went and bought lots of jeans for himself.

Long before DVRs and on-demand programs, my family and I had some television shows we'd watch every week. One night in 1989 we had settled down to watch Neil Patrick Harris in *Doogie Howser, MD* and our home phone rang. Mary Lou picked it up and discovered it was Larry wanting to talk to me about something. As she handed the phone to me she said something like, "but Doogie's coming on." I laughed and Larry and I talked for a short time and I told him I would call him soon. One week later at the exact same time just as the show was coming on, our telephone rang. Mary Lou answered it and she heard Larry say "Mary Lou – Lar'. I can't talk now cause Doogie is coming on," and hung up. She burst out laughing and we have been enjoying that memory ever since.

Larry also created an outgoing message on the answering machine that we used for several years. I didn't ask him to do it, he just did it and put it on a small cassette tape. It went something like this: "From the Edwards Estate in scenic Arlington Heights, this is the house boy speaking. Thomas can't come to the phone because he is busy working on a big business deal. Mary Lou is trying on some gowns sent over by Halston. The kids are writing profanities on the wall and I am taking care of the polo ponies and cleaning the pool. So, leave a message at the tone." Without exception, callers would be laughing when the machine began recording their message.

One day I left home and inadvertently took both my keys and Mary Lou's car and house keys with me. She called the hotline just before Larry signed off and complained she couldn't go anywhere or do anything until I got home. After we hung up, Larry said he'd leave early and take Mary Lou's keys to her on his way home. This was unusual because he very rarely left the radio station early except on days he played golf. He drove to our house and gave Mary Lou her keys and lectured her (with a smile) that "you should have a third set of keys made so I don't ever have to do this again."

Over time Lar shared some embarrassing stories. For example, he told me one about the Corvette he used to own. He said he was headed home one day and needed to find a bathroom. He stopped at the Oasis on the Northwest Tollway. It is now called the Jane Addams Memorial Tollway. The Oasis was the structure built over the roadway. It had fast food restaurants and a gas station with easy access from both sides of the tollway. He parked his Corvette and went inside to use the facilities. When he walked outside, he panicked when he noticed his Corvette was gone! He found a pay phone and called the Illinois State Police to report a stolen car. Officers arrived at the Oasis to get all the information for their report and Larry described the car along with providing the license plate number. One of the officers walked away and returned minutes later and said he spotted the car out in the parking lot. Here's what happened. Larry had entered the Oasis through the northbound door and had actually walked out through the southbound door on the opposite side of the tollway. His car had been where he had parked it all that time. He said he was so embarrassed. I enjoyed teasing him about that for years and we both always got a big laugh over it.

Larry also told me one Halloween some teens in his Palatine neighborhood had vandalized his Corvette while it was parked in his driveway. So, every Halloween after that he'd spend the whole evening cleaning his garage with the lights on to scare off those "juvenile punks."

I don't know when he sold his Corvette, but he eventually drove a Toyota and always parked it at a broken meter on Lower Wacker Drive during his show. There were so many bird droppings that accumulated over time on the car's exterior. He never washed them off so they eventually caused the car's paint to deteriorate. Inside the car, he had countless empty donut bags and coffee cups. I remember one snowy day he asked me to jump out of the car and throw some snow on the windshield so he could see out of it.

I asked why he didn't buy some windshield washer fluid and he said it was a waste of money.

Several years ago at a personal appearance, Larry and Jude met a mother with a special needs child. The mother was the only caregiver for her daughter. The two were big fans of Larry and over time the four of them became close friends. Larry and Jude welcomed them into their private lives. After Larry retired, he and Jude moved to New Mexico and the friendship took on a new arrangement. Larry told me that he would fly to Chicago every year to give the mother a break in her daily routine of caring for her daughter by taking the girl back to Santa Fe to spend a couple of weeks at the Lujack home. He told me the girl loved the adventure of being on an airplane and spending time with Larry & Jude. Then the two would fly back to Chicago and, before Larry returned home, he would make sure the pantry and refrigerator were completely stocked with food and essentials.

On my last day at WLS, Larry offered to drive me home and it was during that car trip to Arlington Heights he admitted that he previously had been approached about the two of us teaming up to do the morning show. Instead of agreeing to it, he said he took all the money that had been budgeted for the show for himself. I had been approached by management about teaming up with Larry. They offered me a 10-year contract that was "connected to Larry." It was never made completely clear what that term meant. Larry was a little distant during that time and he never approached me about wanting to team up. I felt the offer wasn't in my best interest since it wasn't presented with a genuine effort. Hearing him admit that he took all the money budgeted for that show confirmed something that I had often wondered about. He obviously felt very guilty. In retrospect, everything worked out for the best. I went on to have many big successes in my career.

We kept in contact after I left WLS and eventually went on to do mornings at WJMK in Chicago and programming jobs in Chicago at WKQX, in Boston at WODS and in Los Angeles at KCBS-FM. A few years after our son Tommy was born, we returned to Chicago for a brief vacation. Also, I had been contacted by a Chicago talent who wanted to leave his morning drive position at one of the very successful FM radio stations and come to Los Angeles to work for me.

I called Larry and asked if we could get together so he could meet Tommy. He invited Mary Lou, Tommy and me to his home in Palatine and we had a great time. Larry established a relationship with Tommy that lasted over the years where he would call our home and if Tommy answered, they'd spend a lot of time talking sports. Larry was very supportive of Tommy's basketball career in high school and college and would call him to hear about his games. He would tell Tommy if he ever planned to run away from home, he'd always be welcome to live with Jude and him in New Mexico. Tommy always said that Larry was like a real uncle to him.

Most of the letters I received from Larry were either handwritten or typed out. Here are a few excerpts from the letters:

It was a handwritten note dated January 2002:

"Hey – wanna see a picture of my grandkids? (attached) The little one is age 5 and is really cute – the big one is 13 and a teenage god! His poor mom has to field phone calls at all hours of the night from every aggressive junior high girl in Boise. The record so far is 1:45am! My inherited DNA continues to turn out fine-looking results."

Here's an excerpt from a letter composed on his prized manual typewriter: (all in upper case, typed on yellow tablet paper including misspelled words)

DEAR TED WARDS

HOW EMBARASSING! I'M OUT OF TYPING PAPER AND I'M NOT SURE WHETHER MY '87 COROLLA (DESCRIBED ON MOST USED VEHICLE LOTS AS AN "ENTRY-LEVEL SHIT CAR") HAS ENOUGH GAS TO MAKE IT DOWN THE MOUNTAIN TO OFFICE DEPOT. AS YOU KNOW, I HAVE NO INTEREST IN THE WEB...AND NO ACCESS TO IT.

(The following was typed in red ink): BUT I'VE GOT A SPIFFY RED RIBBON ON MY SMITH-CORONA SECRETARIAL MODEL #76!!! AND IS THAT HI-TECH OR WHAT????

Most of Larry's letters arrived in the mail but later I'd receive them from his fax machine. Many would include this P.S.: *"Remind young Tom that God gave him elbows for a reason. Use them in rebounding."* Tommy always laughed when I read it to him. He never took it seriously.

During my research I discovered some memos in my WLS file that brought back great memories.

Here is the first and again all in upper case:

Division: Rock'n Roll
To: AIR PERSONALITIES
From: LARRY LUJACK
Date: Feb. 2, 1976
Subject: VACATIONS

AS YOU KNOW, WHEN ONE OF YOU GOES ON VACATION, I HAVE TO WORK ON SATURDAY MORNING THAT WEEK. NORMALLY, I USE SATURDAY MORNINGS TO "RECOVER" FROM THE WEEK BEFORE…I SLEEP LATE…THEN PLAY GOLF IN THE AFTERNOON. FOR THIS REASON, I AM ASKING YOU ALL TO PLEASE KEEP YOUR VACATION TIME TO AN <u>ABSOLUTE</u> MINIMUM. I DON'T SEE ANY NEED FOR ANY OF YOU TO TAKE MORE THAN ONE WEEK OFF PER YEAR. BESIDES CONFUSING OUR LISTENERS, WHO ARE USED TO HEARING US AT THE SAME TIME EVERDAY…VACATIONS ARE EXPENSIVE. BY STAYING ON THE JOB YOU WILL HELP OUR RATINGS…<u>AND</u> KEEP MORE MONEY IN YOUR SAVINGS ACCOUNT.

I RECENTLY RECEIVED MEMOS STATING THAT BOTH BILL PRICE AND TOMMY EDWARDS ARE GOING ON VACATION IN MARCH. THAT MEANS I'M GOING TO HAVE TO WORK ON <u>TWO SATURDAYS IN A ROW!</u> I'M **NOT** A SIDE OF BEEF! I DON'T <u>NEED</u> THIS SHIT! DON'T FUCK ME LIKE THIS! I DON'T THINK I'M ASKING TOO MUCH. THANK YOU IN ADVANCE FOR THE COOPERATION I KNOW I'M GOING TO RECEIVE.

CC: GREENBERG, GEHRON

P.S. TOM AND BILL: IF YOU DECIDED TO CANCEL YOUR MARCH VACATIONS, PLEASE LE ME KNOW AS SOON AS POSSIBLE. (IF I DON'T HEAR FROM YOU BY TOMORROW…YOU CAN GUESS ABOUT

HOW MANY TIMES I'M GOING TO BE PASSING OFF
TO YOU ON FRIDAY NIGHT...ZERO! I WILL BRING
THE BALL UP COURT AND SHOOT EVERY DAMN
TIME...WHETHER I'VE GOT A GOOD SHOT OR
NOT....I'LL PUT IT IN THE AIR.)

In 1981 Program Director Ric Lippincott decided to end using
his professional name and use only his legal name henceforth. First
Ric's memo then Lars':

To: WLS Staff

From: Dave Denver

Date: November 16, 1981

Subject: Name change

I would like to announce my decision to drop the alias
name "Dave Denver" and begin using my birth given name,
Richard Lippincott. While I have grown fond of the name
"Dave", it is not my own and no longer has a purpose. My
family calls me Ric. I dislike "Dick" or "Rich". (No offense
to any with same).

Thank you for adjusting with this personal matter.

Now Lujack's response:

To: WLS STAFF

From: LARRY LUJACK

Dave: Nov. 16, 1982 *(notice he got the date wrong)*

Subject: NAME CHANGE

I WOULD LIKE TO ANNOUNCE MY DECISION
TO DROP MY LEGAL NAME, "LARRY LUJACK" AND
BEGIN USING THE STAGE NAME, DAVE DENVER.
AFTER USING THE NAME FOR 23 YEARS AS A ROCK

SENSATION COAST TO COAST, I HAVE, QUITE FRANKLY, GROWN TIRED OF IT. AND DECIDED TO GLOM ONTO THE "DENVER" NAME WHEN IT RECENTLY (5 MINUTES AGO) BECAME AVAILABLE. I HAVE DECIDED TO GO SHOW-BIZ ALL THE WAY AND ALSO CHANGE MY MIDDLE NAME TO "DYNA-MITE!" DAVE DYNAMITE! DENVER. I DISLIKE THE NAME "DAVE"…(NOT "GLITZY" ENOUGH)…SO YOU CAN CALL ME "D-3"…"DYNO"…"BIG D"…OR MR. DENVER…BUT YA DOESN'T HAVE TO CALL ME JOHNSON.

Then Larry drew three large "D"s with stars all around them and said it was his new logo and he hopes we like it.

I'm sure there was more correspondence and memos but quite frankly the ink has faded and I can't decipher the whole content.

CBS did a major cost-cutting program in 2002, dropping several successful program directors and consolidating responsibilities with other PDs. During that time, I did some consulting work in addition to being program director for American General Media in New Mexico, so I had the chance to spend time with Larry. He offered to drive me around Albuquerque and his new hometown of Santa Fe. While we were in Albuquerque, I looked at some apartments while he waited outside. After looking at one, I came out with two chocolate chip cookies. He asked me where I got them. I told him they were on a plate just inside the door. He got out of the car and went inside and brought back a handful of cookies with a big smile on his face.

Speaking of cookies, I am reminded of a time when former WLS Music Director Steve "Pookie" Perun called me and said he would be in Albuquerque for a couple days consulting a radio station and asked that I contact Larry to set up a dinner. I called Larry and he suggested we meet at one of the big casinos that Friday night. Larry, always ahead in the fashion trends, showed up on time wearing torn jeans and a straw cowboy hat. We all met and went inside to the restaurant. I noticed the security guards kept their eyes on us. Larry offered to buy us dinner. It was an all you can eat fish fry for $11 each and he said he expected us to eat at least $25 worth of food each. So, we gorged ourselves. Then Larry asked Pookie to check the dessert table. He came back to our table and began listing all the goodies on the dessert table: "Cookies, cakes, pies, ice cream, custard and brownies." Larry asked, "Where are they?" "On the table" replied Perun. Larry said, "How come they're not here?" Pookie realized that Larry had sent him to the table to bring samples of everything. He went back and brought a sample of everything he could fit on a tray. Larry stuffed the cookies in his pocket, and we tried to eat what we could. Larry said he was happy we had eaten far more than $11 worth of food each. He said it was "money well spent."

On another day, he picked me up in Albuquerque and we drove up to Santa Fe. I had mentioned I wanted to see the interior of St. Francis Cathedral with its beautiful Spanish décor. He waited outside smoking a cigarette and then it was off to a very popular restaurant for lunch. We sat at a table outside and when the waitress came to our table, I mentioned I wanted an appetizer and a beer. Larry asked for ice cream and a beer. I told the waitress she should refuse that order because no one ever asks for ice cream and a beer. Larry insisted he wanted ice cream and a beer, so she went off to get our food. That got us laughing and then I said something stupid about something that was going on at a nearby table and that set him off. He started laughing so hard which caused me to do the same that we were both doubled over with laughter. I was sure we were going to be asked to leave. Eventually, we settled down and had a nice lunch – at least I did.

We drove around the artist community and wound up back at his home, sitting in his small pickup truck talking about our experiences in the military. I had been in the Navy and he served in the Air National Guard. One thing led to another and he started telling me something that was obviously haunting him. The more he revealed what it was all about, the more emotional he got. I just sat and listened without asking questions or interrupting him. He told me something that had affected him for decades. Out of respect for Larry's privacy, I won't reveal the circumstances of this but believe me this was something that had caused him pain for a long time, and he began sobbing. I felt so bad but I was glad he felt he could trust me with this personal story. I said a few things that hopefully comforted him, and he regained composure. We never talked about it again.

In September of 2012, Larry and I were contacted by Dennis Lyle, President and CEO of the Illinois Broadcasters Association, informing us that we were being honored in Springfield, Illinois with an award from the Illinois Emergency Management Agency. We had done a series of public service announcements about pet safety and pet preparations for emergencies the year before. We encouraged families to not only have emergency supplies for the family but to include supplies for their pets.

One afternoon during this trip, Larry joined Mary Lou and me in our Springfield hotel room to tell stories and laugh about old times.

I gave him a Chicago Bulls cap like the players wore and he gave me a University of New Mexico T-Shirt. He told me he watched Bulls games on television with neighbors and boasted he knew the guy making the announcements. He said, "Now I've got proof."

We had dinner with the executives of the organizations mentioned above. The award ceremony was the next afternoon. Larry and I spent about an hour answering questions and signing autographs for *Animal Stories* fans from all over the state. Mary Lou and I also received a VIP tour of the Abraham Lincoln Presidential Museum. Larry didn't want to go along, because he wanted to catch a flight back to Santa Fe.

I didn't know then that this would be the last time we would see each other.

In early 2013 Larry and I were talking about bringing a version of Animal Stories back. A client of WJMK radio had expressed interest in sponsoring a shortened version of the feature. We were in the primitive discussions of its viability when we had to put everything on hold. Larry discovered he was very ill.

In late January 2013, I was working WJMK in Chicago. I worked on a remote broadcast aboard a Disney cruise ship and returned home to find several messages on my landline answering machine. Larry told me he'd never call me on my cell phone because he didn't trust them. I returned his call late that evening to learn about Larry waking up one recent morning and realizing something was drastically wrong. Jude rushed him to the hospital and the doctors discovered internal bleeding. They were able to control the bleeding and took several tests that resulted in a diagnosis of esophageal cancer. Larry asked me to keep it private. I asked what it meant, and he said the doctors told him he had about a year to live. I was devastated. Larry mentioned I could tell Mary Lou about it but no one else. He said "I don't want anyone calling me saying, "Oh Lar I'm so sorry." I promised I wouldn't. He began having chemotherapy treatments.

He even kept the secret from his aging mother who was in a nursing home in Idaho. He would visit her often and he always wore his straw cowboy hat. She eventually noticed the hair around his ears was missing (a side effect of the chemo treatments) and she asked why. He didn't tell me how much he shared with her.

Larry told me he was spending days going through files, weeding out old papers, locating insurance policies and deciding what was to happen after his death.

Over the last eleven months of his life, Larry and I talked on the telephone once every week to ten days. I would call to check up on him and he would share some of the difficult times he was going through with chemotherapy. In the early days, he didn't mention the negative side effects but as time went by, the stories he would tell made me very sad. I would always change the subject and remind him of something in our history that made us both laugh. I don't know if it did any good, but it made me feel better to hear him chuckle or at least hear what sounded like a smile in his voice and on his face. There was a glimmer of optimism on occasion when he was about to get the results of whether the disease was reacting to the treatment. Then in the next call, he'd share the disappointing news from his doctor. Toward the end, I heard him describe his pain and how uncomfortable he was.

In the last six weeks of his life, he withdrew. He didn't return calls and Jude told me his condition was getting worse. Eventually, she told me hospice had been called in.

On December 18, 2013, the night he died, my cell phone rang. I had a strong feeling it was going to be bad news. Jude was crying when I answered, and it took a little time for her to say the words. There was another long pause as it sunk in. She asked me to keep the news private until the next day because she couldn't handle phone calls. I told her I wouldn't tell anyone except Mary Lou. In less than an hour, John Gehron called me and said he received a call from someone asking if it was true that Larry Lujack had died. I fell silent. He said, "Hello?" I eventually said, "I can't talk about it." He asked if I knew it was true and I repeated that I couldn't talk about it. John said he'd call the person back and say he couldn't reach me. I called Jude right away and she said she had begun getting calls too. I confirmed with her that I had not mentioned it to anyone. She later told me she discovered the news was released by Larry's son Tony in New York. She said it's OK to tell people now that the news is out. Shortly after that a Chicago TV reporter called and asked me to describe what made Larry Lujack's career memorable. I told her she obviously wasn't a Chicagoan and I didn't want to say anything other than he was the best. I knew this was going to happen, but I wasn't prepared to have any kind of statement.

I went into a deep funk following his death. Larry made it clear he wanted no funeral or memorial service. He planned to have his remains donated to the University of New Mexico Medical School for research. Not having a funeral or memorial service kept many of us from saying goodbye to him. And I missed talking to him and laughing with him.

Larry Lujack was a very talented guy with an unusual public personality. It was so obvious he intimidated people wherever he went. I feel fortunate that I had the opportunity to know the private person. He asked me to write, edit and approve the introductions to two major halls of fame. He also asked me to review and approve the inscriptions on both plaques.

I'll always remember the friendship we shared and the laughter we had at work, on the phone and just hanging out together. That made the difficult times a little easier.

CHAPTER 15

A Round of Tequila – The Good Stuff

"Hurt So Good" – John Mellencamp
"Every Breath You Take" – The Police
"How Deep is Your Love" – The Bee Gees

AFTER REAL OLDIES 1690 WRLL WENT BELLY UP IN late summer 2006, I soon heard from two old friends. The first was Steve Schanwald of the Chicago Bulls who invited me to lunch. He told me Steve Scott, who was the Public Address Announcer, had landed a great job in New York at WCBS-AM. Schanwald asked if I'd consider returning to the Bulls as the PA. We worked out a deal before dessert and I accepted.

A few weeks later another old friend, Ric Lippincott of WILV-FM also known as LOVE FM called and invited me to lunch. He said his VP of Programming, Greg Solk would join us. I looked forward to that. We had been friends for a number of years. Greg had worked at WLUP back in the 80s. He was now in charge of programming the Bonneville stations in Chicago. The last time Greg and I had talked was after I launched the Arrow Format in Los Angeles. Over lunch the two asked if I'd do the afternoon show on WILV. I told them I was interested but there was one important detail we had to work out. Doing the afternoon radio show would interfere with me attending pre-game meetings on Bulls game days at the United Center. Plus, I had to have a chance to have dinner before the game. I asked if I could arrange to leave a little early on those days. I would pre-record a few breaks that my relief would play before their shift began. Ric and Greg were very accommodating. They agreed and we were all set.

A few months later the morning talent at WILV unexpectedly decided to leave for a position at a radio station in Los Angeles. This left the morning show open.

By this time, it was early 2007. Barry James had replaced Ric Lippincott as Program Director. With the morning show now open, Greg and "BJ" asked me to move to that time slot. That turned out to be a lot of fun even though I wasn't getting much sleep on Bulls game nights. Anyone who has to get up at 3 a. m. needs to go to bed early in the evening. I wanted to continue to work for the Chicago Bulls so on game days, I needed a nap. Whenever possible I would try to get a 90 minute nap before I went to the United Center for a game. The day after a Bulls game, I needed another nap. Most morning jocks take a nap whenever they have appearances or other obligations at night. So this wasn't all that unusual.

I had a wonderful contract at WILV that I had an agent negotiate for me. I admit now that I am the worst agent for myself. I regret not using an agent in earlier contracts. I've worked on both sides of the desk. I negotiated for myself as talent and on the other side of the equation as a manager living within a company budget. I was a much better negotiator as a manager. Many super successful air-talents have agents that do a great job in representing their clients. One or two guys I know have their wives negotiate for them. I think I should have done that.

It was a pleasure to work at WILV. The air staff included Megan Reed, Susan Wiencek and the three Brians: Brian Peck, Brian Travis and Brian Middleton. Everyone respected the management staff. At that time Bonneville was the parent company of WILV and two other Chicago stations. The company was rated one of the best companies in broadcasting to work for.

While I had a great run at WILV, there were major problems developing around the country that would ultimately affect me. The U.S. economy was diving into a recession. By the fall of 2008, I had the biggest contract of the talent at WILV and it wasn't surprising that the company needed to cut costs. I grew increasingly aware that things were going to change because I actually could see it coming. Being a former PD, I knew what commercials on the air were generating revenue and what commercials were "P.I." spots. A "P.I." commercial is a *personal inquiry* announcement – meaning they only generated real money when listeners called a toll-free telephone number and ordered or inquired about whatever the product or service was. Then the radio station would be rewarded with revenue. That's why these types of commercials run so often. Today as just another listener, I find them all so annoying. The recession affected not only me but several others at the facility. I regretted having to leave WILV because I really enjoyed working there.

So again, I was unemployed in radio but still doing public address announcing at the Bulls games. A couple of months after I left the radio station, Greg Solk approached me at a Bulls game. He said, "We miss you. Why not come back and do some weekend and fill-in work?" I told him I liked the idea so he told me to call Program Director Barry James and talk it over with him.

In early 2009 I was back on the air at WILV working a few weekends a month and filling in for air talent on vacation. The working environment at WILV hadn't changed. The air-staff and management were all veterans and there was a spirit of camaraderie. Barry James was a highly respected professional. He always welcomed me into his office after my shift to talk about upcoming promotions and programming ideas and we'd wind up sharing many radio experiences in our careers. He is a very creative storyteller.

The number of weekend and fill-in shifts for me at WILV dropped considerably over a period of time. There were several part-time announcers on the staff and the work needed to be spread around. At one time I had regular weekly assignments but by January and February of 2011, I averaged only two per month.

In March of that year a familiar set of call-letters contacted me again and I would discover that the third time is indeed the charm.

It was early 2011 that the Chicago Cubs announced they were searching for a new Public Address Announcer. One day the morning team at WBBM-FM called and asked if I'd join them and provide tips on how they could audition for the job. I knew this was going to be fun. I wound up spending about 45 minutes with them on the air having them read PA announcements I wrote. It was hysterical. I'd have them read the scripts over and over again giving them direction each time and they'd still mess things up.

Everyone was laughing, and I told them to stick with their morning show job. After I left the studio, I stopped by the office of Program Director Todd Cavanah to say hello. We had known each other back when I programmed two CBS radio stations. After we got caught up about family and careers, he asked for my contact information.

In early March of 2011, I was having lunch in a sports bar with my friend Ed Marcin watching the opening games of the NCAA Men's Basketball Tournament. My cell phone rang, and it was Todd. He asked, "What's all the noise?" I told him I had trouble hearing him since I was in a bar watching hoops and drinking beer. He asked if I'd be interested in joining WJMK (K-Hits 104.3) as a weekender and fill-in. I said, "I don't know, maybe." He said, "Keep drinking beer, get a little drunk and just say yes." I laughed, and I told him I'd come in and see him on Monday. He said I would have a guarantee of two shifts per week plus lots of fill in and an attractive salary. Later that day I told Mary Lou I'd like to do it. She agreed and that was my **third** go at working at WJMK.

Almost immediately I was very busy working some 7-day weeks. One of the full-time announcers who was doing the afternoon shift spent his on-air time with his computer next to him logged onto a Skype dating site. During the songs he would be interviewing girls who were looking to hook-up. He told me he was inundated with girls wanting to meet him. Because he was using Skype, the girls could watch him do his radio work and they felt like they were a part of his show. He had many other issues he was dealing with and it wasn't long until he was sent on his way.

On another day I got a call from Todd saying the nighttime guy had not shown up for his show and asked if I could get to the radio station quickly. I had been working on some projects at home and

I told him I'd shower and get there as fast as possible. By the time I got to the station, the jock was in the studio and on the air. Todd and another staffer had gone to the guy's apartment and woke him up. Apparently he had been out all night and simply overslept. He also left the station a short time later.

There were more changes happening at the radio station. Todd decided to move the midday air-talent, Gary Spears, into the afternoon shift and he asked me to sign a 2-year agreement to do the midday shift 10 a.m.-2 p.m. After a month or two my show was extended an additional hour to 9 a.m.-2 p.m. Monday through Friday and a show on Sunday. My daily show followed Eddie & JoBo in the Morning. I hung out in the studio with them during their last half hour. These two very talented legends had me laughing every day.

While I was at K-Hits I had the opportunity to do a remote broadcast from a Disney Cruise Ship. We sailed to The Bahamas from Port Canaveral in Florida. Upon arriving in Nassau, we explored the town on foot. During the early days of working full time at K-Hits, I was also very fortunate to do shows at Walt Disney World and other Orlando vacation destinations. Working there was great fun. I was working MY time slot playing MY music and I said so on-the-air. This was the music I personally enjoyed the most.

Two years went by and Todd asked me to sign a new 2-year agreement and it was then I started asking myself about retirement. Mary Lou and I decided to go ahead and sign the new agreement and she said whenever I decided I wanted to retire, she would fully support me.

I really had to wrestle with this decision. But eventually I realized after 54 years of being on the radio or in a management position, I was ready to walk away from radio and enjoy whatever was next. I felt privileged that I was able to retire on my terms.

Once we decided on an effective date, Todd asked me if I'd be interested in doing a remote broadcast from an RV dealer during the last week I was on the air. I said I'd just rather do my last week here in the studio. So he agreed. I played some of my favorite songs and even ran some old *Animal Stories*. On my last day Penny Jackson of the programming staff decorated the studio with old pictures from my career, balloons and congratulatory messages. Mary Lou and Tommy joined me in the studio and it got to be a little emotional toward the end of my show. I thanked not only Todd but also Market Manager Rod Zimmerman, my old program directors and managers and everyone I could think of. I made sure I thanked my daughters Shannon and Amy and son Tommy but most importantly Mary Lou – my bride of 45 years at that time for all her love and sacrifice to enable me to live my dream. By this time my voice was cracking and it was time to say goodbye.

Todd arranged for a dinner at a Mexican Cantina a few nights later and he invited a few of my radio station friends: Bob Lawson, Dave Fogel, Gary Spears and Chris Clybor. I was also delighted to have the Market Manager for CBS, Rod Zimmerman attend. Rod and I had known each other for years. In fact when I was in Los Angeles, he was Market Manager in St. Louis and he invited me to that city to consult the CBS oldies station. It meant so much to me that Rod attended my retirement dinner.

It was a special night of good food, great stories, and many laughs. Eventually Todd called the waiter over and said, "A round of tequila…and make it the good stuff." It was the perfect nightcap. We went our separate ways. I took a commuter train home and

I had the time to reflect on my love for radio and the 54 years I spent living it.

Sometimes I miss being on the radio, but I have no regrets leaving when I did. I had great fun. I made so many good friends and have many wonderful memories.

CHAPTER 16

I'll Be Talkin' To You

"(I've Had) The Time of My Life"
– Bill Medley & Jennifer Warnes

I'VE BEEN VERY LUCKY. I FOUND A GIRL WHO WAS willing and happy to put up with the crazy life of a radio guy. It's a life of moving from town to town and coast to coast. It's a life of having good friends who are going through the same experiences. I've always thought of radio being a small world. I know it's true because I've run into the same people several times over a long career.

For Mary Lou and me, it's been an adventure. And we've shared it with three incredible children.

When we moved from New York to the Chicago area, Shannon, our oldest daughter was born less than 2 months later. We had a small apartment in the Arlington Heights area. About a year after she was born, we moved to a high-rise in downtown Chicago on State Street. We lived there for 3 years and by the time Mary Lou was expecting our second child, we decided to move back to our old neighborhood. We bought our first house in Arlington Heights. Once again, we moved while Mary Lou was pregnant with our daughter Amy who was born at the same hospital as Shannon. The four of us lived in that home until we bought a newly constructed house in the same neighborhood in 1987.

All three of my girls did some modeling work for print ads and television commercials in the 80's. Mary Lou did a TV ad for the First National Bank of Chicago and one for Sears and was an extra in a few other spots.

Shannon's career in television actually began at age 10. She was featured in a commercial for Jewel Foods. In the commercial Shannon, with help from her pretend Mom, shopped at the Jewel supermarket for the ingredients for a meatloaf dinner she'd make for her family. In the next scene she was seen in the kitchen cracking eggs in a bowl, and then she watched her mom take the meatloaf out of the oven. Finally, Shannon carried the entree to the table and said, "Dad, I made it all by myself." Then we heard the jingle: "If it's important to you it's important to Jewel." The first showing of that commercial had a sizable audience. It premiered on *WMAQ-TV*, Chicago on January 30, 1983 right after Super Bowl 17.

Shannon was on the swim team at Buffalo Grove High School and she was also involved in some of the drama programs. During the summer she was a lifeguard at the community pool in our neighborhood. She graduated high school around the time I accepted a programming position from CBS in Boston.

212

Amy, our younger daughter grew up in Arlington Heights, Boston and Los Angeles – what a trooper! Amy was also on television when she was younger. At age 6 she was in a national Cap'n Crunch cereal television commercial. Between her audition for the commercial and the actual shoot, Amy lost a front tooth and we panicked. We knew they wouldn't want a little girl with a tooth missing doing a commercial for a sugared cereal. We called our dentist who asked us to bring her to the office immediately where he made her a "flipper" – a temporary false tooth to replace the missing tooth. No one noticed the difference when the commercial was filmed. She even had a close up with a big smile!

At age 8, Amy had a small role in the theatre production of *Dr. Jekyll and Mr. Hyde* at the Beacon Street Playhouse in Chicago.

Amy started high school in Brookline, a Boston suburb. She was a cheerleader for the Brookline High School hockey team. Hockey is a very popular sport in Boston and yes they have special cheerleaders just for that sport. The family moved to Los Angeles during her sophomore year and she transferred to Calabasas High School.

Another move and again Mary Lou did it when she was pregnant with our third child, Tommy. Our little guy was born only 2 months after we arrived in California.

Both of our daughters graduated college in California. Shannon got her degree at the University of California at Santa Barbara. Amy earned hers at San Diego State University.

While Amy was in college, she took advantage of a Summer Study Abroad program to study at Paris-Sorbonne University. She made a number of friends from various countries in Europe and North Africa and she loved Paris. It was tough for her parents to see her board that plane to France. However, it was an exceptional experience for her.

While Shannon was in college, she worked in the summer as a page at CBS Television City in Hollywood. That job opened the door to *The Wheel of Fortune* television show where she has worked for more than 20 years. Shannon is married to Patrick Bobillo, a very talented writer and artist who created all the artwork for the Animal Stories CDs. Shannon and Pat have given us 3 incredible grandchildren, Jenny, Ray and Jimmy.

During Amy's college career, she worked for CBS Television primarily for *The Price Is Right* television show. Upon graduation she worked full-time for the network. She married Brendan Smith who is a very talented visual effects artist for TV commercials, music videos and movies. They have given us our youngest grand-child, Julia who is such a delight!

Our son Tommy was born in Los Angeles when Shannon and Amy were 19 and 15 respectively. You can imagine how surprised they were when we told them we were going to have another baby. We were still living in the Boston area when we discovered Mary Lou was pregnant and we held a family meeting to announce our new addition to the family. We said, "We have something to tell you" and they both groaned and said, "We're moving again." That's a typical reaction in a family where a parent is on the radio. We said, "No, we're going to have another baby" and they both looked at us and reacted with surprise, but you could see it in their eyes "Ewwwww", realizing how it happened. We reminded them that we were even more surprised, but also very happy and excited.

The day Tommy was born, I took Mary Lou to the hospital and parked in the emergency room parking lot. Once I got her to the maternity ward, I went out and moved the car to the regular lot. When I walked down the hallway in the maternity ward, I noticed a man walking towards me. The closer he got the more familiar he looked. We made eye contact and we greeted each other with our first names. It was Walt "Baby" Love, whom I had worked with at WOR-FM in New York. Walt asked, "What are you doing here?" I told him Mary Lou was having a baby boy. He told me his wife Sonia was about to give birth to their son. The two moms met later in recovery separated by a curtain. Our two boys, Stephan and Tommy were born within an hour and twenty minutes of each other. *The Los Angeles Times* in their Valley Edition several days later carried a photo of the boys and their proud dads with a story about a great reunion.

I got back from running into Walt just in time to put on a gown and a mask and be with Mary Lou when our son came into the world.

Having Tommy when we did gave us the opportunity to meet new people, make new friends and experience things in life that we might have missed out on. He grew up in both Los Angeles and the Chicago area. He played basketball all four years at Lake Forest High School and also at the College of Lake County where he was Captain of the team. He was a ball boy for the Chicago Bulls for 9 seasons where he had the opportunity to assist NBA Players and coaches. During those shoot-arounds he was asked to help future Hall of Fame players including Kevin Durant and Tim Duncan in their workouts.

Tommy graduated from California State University Northridge and currently works for Evolution Media. Some of their productions include "*The Real Housewives of Beverly Hills*" and "*Vanderpump Rules*" among others. It looks like there is a pattern here. Their dad was in radio and they all went into television!

It doesn't really surprise us that they all went into broadcasting. When our daughters were growing up and Shannon was in middle school and Amy in elementary school, I used to take them to work with me at WLS Radio on Saturdays. While I was on the air in Studio A, they'd be in Studio B pretending to be on the air. One was the announcer and the other was the board-operator. I couldn't hear them but it was fun to watch. Later both girls had actual jobs at radio stations. Shannon answered phones and produced the Saturday and Sunday night shows for Little Walter (DeVenne) at WODS-FM in Boston. Amy worked in the promotion department at KCBS-FM – Arrow 93 – in Los Angeles one summer.

Tommy worked in the promotion department at WJMK-FM – K-HITS – in Chicago one summer. He represented the radio station at appearances including recording listeners' comments that were used on the air. He also had administrative duties including making travel arrangements for contest winners.

Tommy worked for TheCube.com, a company that broadcasts high school basketball games on the internet. He did play-by-play of games in the Chicago area and for a special holiday tournament in Palm Desert, California. During his time as a ball boy for the Bulls, Tommy met 3 of the legendary national play-by-play broadcasters including Marv Albert, Kevin Harlan and Mike Breen.

Mary Lou's mother Louise used to say, "Children are a special gift from God." And we were given three very special gifts.

I'm also thankful for the chance to travel both on business and pleasure to places that hold many memories. After our honeymoon in St. Croix, Mary Lou and I couldn't wait to return to that area. We spent time on several other islands in the Caribbean over the course of many years.

We were able to take our daughters to England and France. We arrived in London the day after Christmas which is called Boxing Day. We asked at least a dozen locals what Boxing Day was and got a dozen different answers. We were in Paris for a few days on that same trip. We spent New Year's Eve on the Champs-Elysees and talk about a party!

We've visited with radio people in Malmo, Sweden, Cambridge, U.K. and Amsterdam, where I had the opportunity to speak at an international radio conference. We took our son with us on that trip and the 3 of us hopped on a train to visit Brussels. The train was going to Paris with a short stop in Brussels...a very short stop. As we were about to get off, it started to move and we had to jump off. We have also spent some time in Copenhagen, Lucerne and Zurich, Switzerland.

When our son Tommy was in grade school, we attended the school gala and auction and bid on a trip to Spain. We were lucky to win that trip and the three of us spent Easter Sunday in Madrid that year. We drove throughout Spain and enjoyed seeing the Straits of Gibraltar and spending time on the Spanish Riviera. The beaches of the Mediterranean are topless. I think our 8-year-old son noticed. I know I did!

And of course, because of my job and the different moves we have made, we've travelled up and down the Atlantic Coast, Midwest, Southwest and Pacific Coast of the U.S. There are so many beautiful places to see right here at home in the U.S and we plan on seeing many more.

Mary Lou and I are so fortunate to have made many friends not only in Chicago and Los Angeles but all over the country.

Both Larry Lujack and Marty Greenberg told me about the wonderful life experience of being a grandfather. They were so right. We have been able to enjoy Little League baseball games, school musicals, graduations from pre-school and middle school so far. I know there will be many more celebrations as my family grows.

When I reflect on our moves and the timing of them, I realize the great sacrifice Mary Lou experienced in moving during critical times. While many radio people moved much more often than we did, it's still unfair to ask a wife to move when she is carrying a child. But she did it because I wanted her to. I'll never forget her love and devotion to make me happy.

Thanks for reading my stories. If you grew up listening to me, you probably heard how I ended each show on the radio.

"Thanks for listening. I'll be talkin' to you."

Made in the USA
Monee, IL
26 April 2020